D1226468

Usonia, **NEW YORK**

Usonia, **NEW YORK**

Building a Community with Frank Lloyd Wright

ROLAND REISLEY *with John Timpane*
Foreword by **MARTIN FILLER**

PRINCETON ARCHITECTURAL PRESS, NEW YORK

PUBLISHED BY
PRINCETON ARCHITECTURAL PRESS
37 EAST SEVENTH STREET
NEW YORK, NEW YORK 10003

For a free catalog of books, call 1.800.722.6657.
Visit our web site at www.papress.com.

Printed in China
04 03 02 01 5 4 3 2 1 First edition

Frontispiece: Detail of Frank Lloyd Wright's 1947 original site plan of Usonia.

Editing and layout: Clare Jacobson
Design: Deb Wood

This publication was supported in part with funds from the New York State Council on the Arts, a state agency.

Special thanks to: Nettie Aljian, Ann Alter, Amanda Atkins, Janet Behning, Jan Cigliano, Jane Garvie, Judith Koppenberg, Mark Lamster, Nancy Eklund Later, Brian McDonald, Anne Nitschke, Evan Schoninger, Lottchen Shivers, and Jennifer Thompson of Princeton Architectural Press—Kevin C. Lippert, publisher

Library of Congress Cataloging-in-Publication Data
Reisley, Roland, 1924–
Usonia, New York : building a community with Frank Lloyd Wright / Roland Reisley with John Timpane ; foreword by Martin Filler.
p. cm.
ISBN 1-56898-245-3
1. Usonian houses—New York (State)—Pleasantville. 2. Utopias—New York (State)—Pleasantville—History. 3. Architecture, Domestic—New York (State)—Pleasantville. 4. Wright, Frank Lloyd, 1867–1959—Criticism and interpretation. i. Title: Usonia. ii. Timpane, John Philip. iii. Title.
NA7238.P54 R45 2001
2001000609

TABLE OF CONTENTS

ACKNOWLEDGMENTS

I could not have produced this account, fourteen years in the making, without significant help. Surely credit is due to the early Usonians who typed and mimeographed—and saved—the thousands of single-spaced communications during the creation and growth of Usonia. (Analogous communications today, much of it by e-mail, or stored on magnetic media, is not likely to survive fifty years.) The Frank Lloyd Wright Archives was another valuable resource.

My friend "Pete" Guerrero contributed beautiful historic photographs and encouraged my efforts, but also introduced me to Dixie Legler. I was at an impasse until Dixie came on to edit my words and to help me integrate some of John Timpane's well-crafted text. She has my gratitude.

For transforming a final draft to this completed text, I thank my editor, Clare Jacobson. Her enthusiastic participation made it happen.

A much appreciated grant from the New York State Council on the Arts helped to pay some of the costs of this project.

Decidedly not least, I thank my wife Ronny, who endured my preoccupation with this history and offered informed comment on much of the text.

I am grateful to the many Usonians who shared their memories of the struggles and triumphs in the life of Usonia, and especially to David and Priscilla Henken, Judy and Odif Podell, Aaron and Millie Resnick, Herbert Brandon, and Rowland Watts, without whose commitment Usonia may not have succeeded.

FRANK LLOYD WRIGHT VISITS USONIA, 1949.

HENRY RAPISARDA, COSMO-SILEO ASSOCIATES

Martin Filler **FOREWORD**

COMMISSIONING A BUILDING BY FRANK LLOYD WRIGHT WAS SUCH AN EXTRAORDINARY EXPERIENCE THAT OVER THE YEARS SEVERAL OF HIS CLIENTS HAVE WRITTEN REVEALING MEMOIRS ABOUT THEIR ADVENTURES WITH THE MASTER, WHICH SOME HAVE REGARDED AS THE OUTSTANDING EVENT OF THEIR LIVES. MULTIPLE VOLUMES OF PUBLISHED CORRESPONDENCES SHED FURTHER LIGHT ON WRIGHT'S RELATIONS WITH OTHER OF HIS PATRONS. THOSE VARIOUS ACCOUNTS ARE ALIKE IN THEIR REITERATION OF THE VERY SIMILAR

roller-coaster course of emotions—admiration, adoration, exhilaration, exasperation, resignation, expectation, and ultimate fulfillment—that Wright's clients went through in the arduous process of bringing his singular designs to reality.

In 1947 (the year that large-scale construction resumed in the United States after wartime restrictions on rationed materials and nonessential building were finally lifted) Wright turned eighty. Though he had been a nationally and internationally acclaimed architect for almost half a century, only during the postwar period did his workload finally catch up with his fame. Whole decades of his exceptionally long career had been blighted by circumstances both within and beyond his control. In the 1910s a shift in fashionable taste away from the arts-and-crafts movement and toward the colonial revival eroded his Midwestern client base, as did the scandal he caused by abandoning his wife and six children to run off with the wife of a client. The 1920s witnessed Wright's attempt to reestablish his practice in Southern California and the Southwest, with just a few houses completed and several major projects that came to naught. The onset of the Great Depression only deepened his woes, and he retreated to Taliesin to found an academy that seemed his last best hope for survival. Wright's wholly unexpected resurgence in the late 1930s, with his astonishing trio of late masterpieces—Fallingwater, the Johnson Wax Building, and Taliesin West—returned him to the forefront of his profession, though World War II soon put an end to his prospects here and abroad.

Wright always had a deep understanding of the national psyche, which is one reason why his work speaks

VIEW FROM THE BALCONY OF THE REISLEY HOME, 1997.

THOUGH REISLEY AND HIS FELLOW COOPERATORS IN THE DEVELOPMENT OF USONIA WERE ATTRACTED TO THE WRIGHTIAN AESTHETIC AND THE MASTER'S BELIEF THAT A HOUSE MUST BE ONE WITH ITS SETTING, THEY WERE ALSO POSSESSED OF A KEEN SOCIAL INSIGHT THAT MAKES THEIR EFFORT ALL THE MORE ADMIRABLE.

to a vast American public in a way that no other architect's does. He was a true Jeffersonian in his inherent distrust of the city and his belief that the basic building block of our democracy must be the freestanding private house. Since the early 1900s Wright cherished the idea of designing affordable housing for the masses; he published plans for low-cost residences in popular magazines, even while he produced his epochal Prairie Houses—richly detailed, labor-intensive, and costly—for an upper-middle-class clientele.

The fallow years of the 1930s gave Wright ample time to rethink the question of the modern suburban house, culminating in his plans for Broadacre City, a low-rise, low-density vision of hypothetical exurban development, as well as in his first Usonian houses. Those radically simplified structures represented Wright's intuitive response to the future direction of domestic architecture in the U.S. (hence the name Usonian) during and after the Great Depression, when even the rich sought to live less ostentatiously. Abandoning the late Victorian formality that marked his epochal Prairie Houses (with their requisite dining rooms, basements, stables or garages, and servants' quarters), he advocated a much simplified format (with small dining areas, concrete-slab construction, carports, and no provision for domestic help) that accurately predicted the nature of postwar family life. His insights into suburbanization were particularly prescient. Indeed, many of Wright's principles—from the private automobile as preferred mode of transportation to the conviction that a new generation of homebuyers would be more receptive to modern architecture—were appropriated by commercial real-estate developers who quickly debased them, to their great profit and the detriment of the landscape.

Just as Wright had attracted a clientele of adventuresome self-made technocrats in turn-of-the-century Chicago and its environs, so did his work appeal to those who, after the upheaval of World War II, wanted to remake their world in a more idealistic image. Wright's ubiquity as a colorful media personality and his carefully crafted persona as a homespun American character encouraged several young admirers to approach him with requests that he design houses for them. The architect was especially intrigued by the proffer to create an entire suburban subdivision in Westchester County, north of New York City, to be called Usonia in homage to his new residential concept.

Roland Reisley, one of the active participants in that project and the author of this account of Usonia and the house he and his wife, Ronny, built there, can be counted among the most important of Wright's clients.

What he lacked in the economic resources of Aline Barnsdall, Edgar Kaufmann, Sr., and Herbert F. Johnson, Jr., Reisley more than made up in commitment and willingness to immerse himself in the technical aspects of Wright's architecture. More than fifty years after he first contacted Wright, this ideal patron now devotes his considerable expertise to the material problems of preserving Wright's built legacy.

Though Reisley and his fellow cooperators in the development of Usonia were attracted to the Wrightian aesthetic and the master's belief that a house must be one with its setting, they were also possessed of a keen social insight that makes their effort all the more admirable. This was not some rarefied artistic exercise, but rather an earnest attempt by a remarkable group of like-minded citizens to use the work of America's greatest architect as the basis for establishing a more fulfilling community life than any of them had known before. Their long-term success, attested to by the fact that the children of several of the original Usonians have returned to live there, is all the more extraordinary given the centripetal demographics of American life over the past half century.

That Wright's participation in Usonia turned out to be less than Reisley and his cohorts had originally intended in no way diminishes the significance of this story. If anything, the variety of architectural responses that the community has been able to absorb is testimony to the adaptability of Wright's ideas, which remain applicable even in the absence of the master's hand. The reverent attitude that Wright's work inspires can be readily translated, as we read in these pages, into action for making better communities for average people, if only the imagination and dedication so vividly documented here is allowed to flourish at large in the land.

PREFACE

50th Anniversary
USONIA HOMES - A COOPERATIVE, INC.
July 30, 1994

ON JULY 31, 1994, TWO HUNDRED AND FIFTY PEOPLE GATHERED FOR A REUNION NEAR THE VILLAGE OF PLEASANTVILLE IN WESTCHESTER COUNTY, NEW YORK. THE GATHERING HAD ALL THE MARKS OF A FAMILY REUNION. KIDS SPLASHED IN THE SWIMMING POOL; A LARGE-SCREEN TV PLAYED VIDEOS OF HOME MOVIES; NEWSPAPER CLIPPINGS WERE CLUSTERED TOGETHER ON A HISTORY WALL; A BIG-TOP TENT ARCHED OVER A COMMUNAL BANQUET. EVERYONE, IT SEEMED, WAS TALKING AT ONCE ABOUT POLITICS, ABOUT THE PAST AND present, about who was dead, who was alive, who was elsewhere. But this was no family reunion, at least not in the biological sense. The occasion was the fiftieth anniversary of the founding of Usonia Homes, A Cooperative Inc., better known as simply "Usonia." Initiated by David Henken, its founders sought to build a modern cooperative community with the guidance and participation of Frank Lloyd Wright.

Between 1948 and 1956 forty-four homes were built on a ninety-seven acre tract of rolling, wooded countryside about an hour's drive from New York City. Three homes were built later, the last in 1963. Frank Lloyd Wright laid out the circular one-acre home sites and the serpentine roads that connected them, and he sketched a proposed community center and farm unit. Initially the houses were cooperatively owned, and all were individually designed, three by Wright. Most of the others were by Wright apprentices and disciples, with his approval. Seven were by other "not necessarily Usonian" architects.

Of the three built communities designed by Wright, including Parkwyn Village and Galesburg Country Homes in Michigan, Pleasantville's Usonia succeeded beyond all expectations, except perhaps Wright's. In over forty years only twelve homes changed hands, six to next-generation Usonians. There were just two divorces. Members became so attached to their houses, their land and their community that even when their needs changed—more children, more money, etc.—rather than move, they built additions. Usonians have enjoyed a remarkable quality of life, the sense of living in an extended family in beautiful homes particularly related to their natural surroundings. But age takes its toll and at this

FIFTIETH ANNIVERSARY CELEBRATION OF USONIA, JULY 31, 1994.

THE THOUSANDS OF PAGES OF DOCUMENTARY RECORDS SAVED OVER THE YEARS—NEWSPAPER ARTICLES, HISTORIC PHOTOS, MINUTES OF MEETINGS, LETTERS, ETC.—ILLUMINATE THE EVENTS, PROBLEMS, AND PASSIONS OF A DEMOCRATIC GROUP CREATING A COMMUNITY.

writing, in 2000, more homes are changing hands. Maintaining the "connectedness" of the original members is a challenge.

Wright's participation and the existence of Usonia have been noted in many books and articles. Over the years thousands of architects, scholars, planners, and students as well as an interested public have visited, admired the community, and urged that a detailed and accurate history of Usonia, its background, and creation be written. Usonians, proud of their experience and wanting to share it, found that imperfect memory, differing recollections of events, and the absence of "organized" documentation prevented even a skeletal account to be presented with confidence. (Prodigious documentation existed, but it was decidedly not organized.) As the long-time secretary of Usonia and de facto historian, I began to prepare a documented account of Usonia and to create an archive for future scholarly study. The thousands of pages of documentary records saved over the years—newspaper articles, historic photos, minutes of meetings, letters, etc.—illuminate the events, problems, and passions of a democratic group creating a community.

The task of organizing, copying, preserving, transcribing, let alone studying these materials has been daunting. Through the active support of Samuel Resnick, a member of Usonia for many years, John Timpane, an accomplished professional writer, also joined the effort to produce this book. His contribution is drawn mainly from recent conversations with Usonia members. Not surprising, the recollections and reminiscences of Usonians after forty to fifty years tend to emphasize a pride and satisfaction with their quality of life, close friendships, joyous events, and a sense of community. The difficulties faced by the group that would eventually build Usonia and the problems later experienced, though mentioned by some, seem minimized or forgotten or, for the last members to join and build, largely unknown.

Historians have observed that oral history, though invaluable, often is not history. While recording interviews with early members, I tried to elicit informative accounts of their discovery of Usonia, their experiences choosing an architect, building a house, and living in the community, and of the problems they dealt with along the way. In 1983 Johanna Cooper, who had joined Usonia in 1973, recorded interviews with a number of members as part of her anthropology thesis. Together, all of these interviews make up a valuable record that will be available for interpretation one day by scholars.

Examination of the documented history, compared with these personal stories, however, reveals omissions, oversights, and errors. One may rightly wonder if such discrepancies are significant. Is it not enough that after fifty years Usonia remains a beautiful place with some fine architecture and an unusually stable membership that feels strongly bonded to Usonia and to each other? Not in the view of many architects, historians, planners, and students among the thousands of visitors who, despite the existence of a handful of other, long-lasting housing communities, see Usonia as unique. There are many beautiful housing developments and fine homes in America. Lifelong friendships among suburban neighbors are not unusual. However, the "connectedness," almost as a family, of *all* Usonians, the wooded land and narrow serpentine roads, and the visible presence and influence of Frank Lloyd Wright are, it seems, atypical and significant.

Nearly all of the many visitors to Usonia come to see the work of Frank Lloyd Wright. When pressed into service as their guide, I always point out that while four hundred Wright-designed buildings still exist in the world, Usonia is unique. Fully assessing the effects of Wright's participation will continue to challenge scholars. However, one of the three Wright-designed homes in Usonia is mine. I have devoted an epilog to the memorable, revealing experiences my wife and I had working with Wright during the design and construction of our home.

Usonians, proud of their accomplishment, hope their story may inform the hopes and efforts of others.

INTRODUCTION

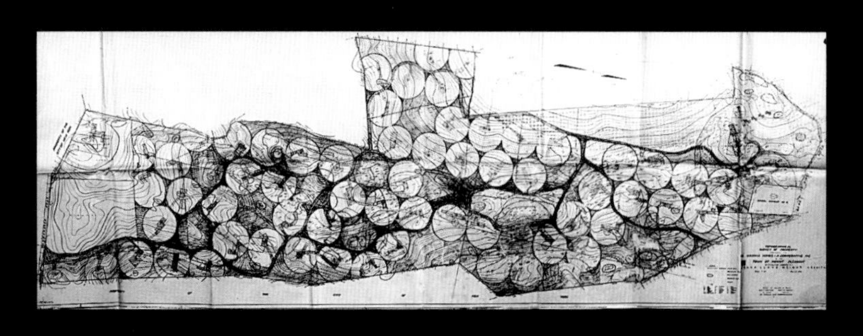

THE CREATION OF USONIA IS A FASCINATING AND WHOLLY AMERICAN STORY. IT IS A ROMANTIC TALE OF A GROUP OF IDEALISTIC, YOUNG URBAN FAMILIES, WHO, FOLLOWING WORLD WAR II, PURSUED THE AMERICAN DREAM OF OWNING A MODERN, AFFORDABLE HOME IN THE COUNTRY. IT IS THE STORY OF THE UNFORESEEN AND NEARLY OVERWHELMING INVESTMENT OF TIME, ENERGY, AND MONEY THAT THESE YOUNG FAMILIES EXPENDED TO CREATE THE UNIQUE COMMUNITY IN WHICH THEY LIVED. THEY NAMED THEIR COMMUNITY of forty-seven homes near Pleasantville, New York, "Usonia" in homage to Frank Lloyd Wright, whose ideas on the way Americans should live together guided their plan. Wright coined the word some thirty years before.

Usonia's story opens in the early 1940s with a group of young New York City professionals. All were in their twenties and all were interested in owning their own homes—but not, if they could help it, in New York City. In 1939 David Henken, a founder of the community, had been talking with friends for several years about forming a cooperative community. In 1940 Henken and his wife Priscilla attended an exhibit of Wright's work at the Museum of Modern Art that changed everything for them. The exhibit included Wright's plan for Usonia I, a cooperative community in Michigan, and a model of Broadacre City. With its acre of land for every family and its faith that the proper ground and proper dwelling could transform the lives of the dweller, Broadacre City planted the ideas that would later take root in Pleasantville.

Indeed, Broadacre City was Wright's master plan for a new American settlement that would restore individuality and worth to the human soul. Wright believed that "a more livable life demands a more livable building under the circumstance of a more living city." Henken later said that seeing Broadacre City at MoMA seemed to "affirm the ideas of a cooperative association" of which he had dreamed. To realize their dream, Henken and his wife left New York and headed to Spring Green, Wisconsin, to become apprentices to Frank Lloyd Wright at his home, Taliesin. Through Henken's efforts, Wright was enlisted to develop Usonia's site plan.

FRANK LLOYD WRIGHT'S ORIGINAL SITE PLAN FOR USONIA, 1947.

COURTESY THE FRANK LLOYD WRIGHT FOUNDATION, SCOTTSDALE, AZ.

The Henkens began a word-of-mouth campaign which soon grew to find others interested in joining them to create a cooperative community of modern houses, and later to seek land on which to build. But land was not easy for them to find, modernist houses were not easy to build, nor were they as affordable as they hoped. And financing, as it turned out, was nearly impossible to secure, especially for a cooperative. But in the end Usonia was created. Ground was broken for the first home in June 1948, and, despite nearly catastrophic upheavals, the community was nearly fully settled by the late 1950s.

Usonia's story involves not only the people who created it and lived in it, but it also reflects the spirit of the times. Many of the most important events of that half century found analogues in Usonia: the cooperative movement, the growth of modern architecture, the Red Scare, and the civil rights movement. The story begins at the close of World War II, when young people were eager to own their own homes, when new technologies were being explored at a rapid rate, and when people were buoyed up by a feeling that ideals could be achieved and risks could be taken. World War II had placed many dreams and all building on hold. The dark, anxious years, however, had a positive side. Americans experienced unprecedented unity of spirit and purpose culminating in the euphoria of the victory of good over evil. Many felt that the momentum of these optimistic feelings would continue in other aspects of life and society—and for a while they did.

For many, society needed more than perfecting, it needed an overhaul. As Usonian Millie Resnick put it, "You have to remember that a lot of things had been going wrong for a long time in this country. There were all sorts of ideas around about how to change things, how to create more justice in society." None of this is to say that Usonians were left-wing radicals, though that was the reputation they would come to have in Pleasantville. As a group, however, they shared liberal ideals. They also shared an optimism that things were going to get better. Most of the early Usonians were not wealthy; many had to struggle to make ends meet for many years. Some were returning veterans trying to put a life together after the war. Others found themselves frozen in jobs that did not pay enough. But their belief—that pretty soon there would be prosperity—fueled the quixotic urge these people had to join forces.

Usonia has never been incorporated into any town or settlement. In the technical/legal sense it is not the name of a place. It is, rather, a focus of people's hopes and aspirations, a center where their selves reside. "We were different," said Usonian Barbara Wax. To be different; to live in harmony with one's surroundings; to be part of a community of caring neighbors—many Americans share that dream. Usonia is the story of people who had an idea and did something to realize it.

Minutes of General Membership Meeting
of Usonia Homes--A Cooperative, Incorporated

January 28, 1945

The general membership of Usonia Homes--A Cooperative, Inc. held a meeting at 255 West 88th Street, New York City, on January 28, 1945 at 8:30 P.M. of that day. There were present in person Priscilla Henken, David Henken, Benjamin Henken, Frieda Henken, Judeth Henken, Irving Medwin, Clarisse White, Lawrence White, Bernard Kessler, George Fox, Alice Stark, Irwin Stark.

On motion duly made and adopted Mr. Medwin was elected temporary chairman and Miss Judeth Henken temporary secretary of the meeting.

The chairman advised the membership of the incorporation of Usonia Homes. He then read the By-laws, after which a discussion followed, and the laws were voted upon, and accepted or amended separately. Article IV, section 3 was amended to read: "Every applicant for a home must be a member of the cooperative." On motion duly made and adopted Article IV, section 3 was accepted as amended. Article IV, section 5 was amended to read: "If charges against a member are found to be warranted, such charges must then be subject to approval by 3/4 of the membership. However, the Board may drop charges if it so desires." On motion duly made and adopted Article IV, section 5 was accepted as amended. Article VII, section 7 was amended to read: "There shall be appointed by the Board of Directors a building committee. This committee shall be responsible for the design, planning, construction, and supervision of all physical and [illegible] structures, etc.... The committee shall also include the [illegible] architects of the corporation who shall be compensated as such on the basis of the prescribed rates recognized by the American Institute of Architects (excluding the cost of land.)

On motion duly made and adopted the By-Laws were accepted

MINUTES OF FIRST MEETING OF USONIA HOMES FOLLOWING INCORPORATION, JANUARY 28, 1945. *COLLECTION ROLAND REISLEY*

Chapter One DREAMING OF USONIA

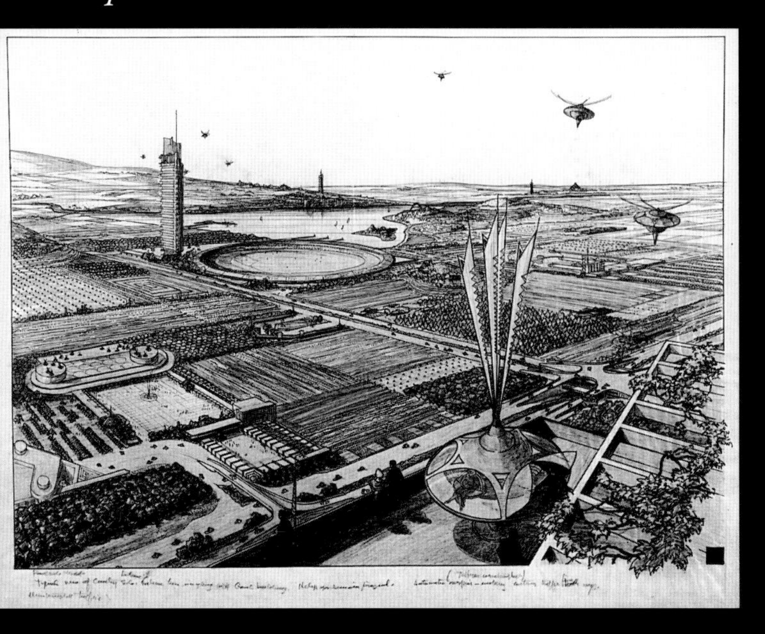

IN THE 1930S AMERICANS ALL ACROSS THE COUNTRY DREAMED OF A BETTER LIFE. THE HARDSHIP OF THE GREAT DEPRESSION LAID BARE THE FAULTS OF A STRICTLY CAPITALISTIC ECONOMY, AND MANY AMERICANS SOUGHT GREATER SOCIAL AND ECONOMIC FAIRNESS. FRANKLIN D. ROOSEVELT'S NEW DEAL "SOCIALISM" WAS ACCORDED AN UNPARALLELED ELECTORAL LANDSLIDE IN 1936. LABOR UNIONS STRENGTHENED AND BECAME MORE PREVALENT IN THE 1930S. AND CONSUMER COOPERATIVES, ONCE MAINLY FARM AND industry groups, grew in popularity as Americans joined shoulder-to-shoulder for mutual benefit

Many young people coming of age in the 1930s felt that life would be much better in the future despite the economic hard times—or perhaps in response to them. Popular culture reinforced this futuristic theme. Kids listened to *Buck Rogers* and *Flash Gordon* on the radio and read futurists Jules Verne and H. G. Wells.

For many, certainly for New Yorkers who had easy access to it, the 1939–40 World's Fair epitomized the optimism that a new, modern, better world was "just around the corner." The major corporations unveiled all manner of technological wonders there: television, robots, fluorescent lighting, FM radio, kitchens of the future with automatic appliances to dazzle the housewife and simplify her chores, and much more. Leading industrial designers, such as Raymond Loewy, Donald Deskey, Russell Wright, Henry Dreyfuss, and others, enhanced most of these innovations. And there was art. Many buildings incorporated the work of fine contemporary artists: Stuart Davis, Fernand Leger, Willem de Kooning, Maksim Gorky, Salvador Dali, Isamu Noguchi, and others. Art and technology seemed to reinforce each other.

The unparalleled highlight of the fair was the General Motors Futurama, a ride over a dramatic model of a future America. The Futurama, designed by architect Norman Bel Geddes, strongly recalled Frank Lloyd Wright's idealized American community, Broadacre City (1930–32), with its decentralized cities, towns, and farms enhanced and connected by advanced highways. Wright presented Broadacre City on April 15, 1935, at Rockefeller Center in New York and then took it on a national speak-

FUTURISTIC DRAWING BY FRANK LLOYD WRIGHT PUBLISHED WITH HIS BROADACRE CITY DISSERTATION *COURTESY THE FRANK LLOYD WRIGHT FOUNDATION, SCOTTSDALE, AZ*

ing tour. His 144-square-foot replica of a model settlement represented a summation of architectural, political, and philosophical ideas. Modern architecture often went hand-in-hand with modern social programs, a faith in progress, and the promise of new technologies, and Wright seemed particularly well positioned to transform new technologies into living spaces that would benefit everyday life.

FRANK LLOYD WRIGHT IN THE 1930S

In the early 1940s it was not necessary to know a lot about architecture to be aware of Frank Lloyd Wright and his buildings. Fallingwater (1935), the Johnson Wax Administration Building (1936), and Taliesin West (1937) received wide publicity in popular magazines, and even his small, affordable "Usonian" houses received some notice. Thanks in large part to Wright, "modern architecture"—like modern music, theater, or film—was something a reasonably well-educated middle-class person could "follow." Wright's work from 1935–41 cemented his name permanently in the American pantheon. If Wright is still, today, the only architect that a significant number of Americans can name, these years were the reasons.

Wright began the decade bankrupt and with his practice at a standstill. (Only two Wright houses were built between 1928 and 1935.) Yet this decade contained his greatest effort to consolidate, redefine, and publicize his architectural practice. In 1932, encouraged by his wife Olgivanna, Wright started the Taliesin Fellowship, a training program for young architects at his Wisconsin home. Also in that year he published *The Disappearing City* and *An Autobiography*, which stimulated new attention for his ideas.

From 1937 to 1941 major articles on Wright appeared in many high-profile periodicals, including *Saturday Review, Scientific American, The Christian Science Monitor Magazine, The Nation, The New Republic,* and *The Science News Letter.* In 1938 both *Architectural Forum* and *Time* featured Wright, dubbing him the "nation's greatest architect." More than any single image, the cover of *Time*, featuring him in a pose of artistic concentration, announced him as a genius and, more importantly, an American genius.

Wright's theme—that the average working family might one day live a modern life in a modern house, in new harmony with nature—was very attractive to the readers of the 1930s. In his Usonian home he dedicated himself to the specific challenge of building for the middle class, creating a house in a cost range accessible to most home-buying Americans while still being worthwhile as an architectural entity. Though he never fully succeeded in designing a home that was truly reasonable for a middle-class purse, his attempt was important. "Usonia" in Wright's mind was to be the quintessential American settlement of the future—an autonomous suburban community expressing the moral harmony of organic architecture.

A PLACE IN THE COUNTRY

While Wright was conjuring plans for a modern new American settlement, David and Priscilla Henken, a young industrial engineer and a school teacher living in New York City, were dreaming of the day when they might build their own home, away from the hustle and bustle of Manhattan. They discussed their plans with several like-minded friends, talking about ways to pool their money to buy land in common, build their own community, and use a common architect and a common builder.

THE NEW YORK WORLD'S FAIR OF 1939–40 EMBODIED THE SPIRIT OF QUINTESSENTIAL AMERICAN TRAITS: OPTIMISM AND FUTURISM.

NEW YORK WORLD'S FAIR, AERIAL VIEW WITH SNOW, 1939, MUSEUM OF THE CITY OF NEW

As Henken put it later, their main motive at first was urban anomie: "In 1939, a group of us living in New York City wanted to move out. The city was too congested, and we wanted more space." The Henkens shared this desire with many of their age and class. "Everyone wanted a place in the country with easy access to the city."

One alternative to urban life was exurban cooperative living. The cooperative movement was reaching its peak around 1940 as a reaction to a strictly capitalistic system. Consumer cooperatives were seen as practical methods to achieve economic benefits—whether buying groceries or housing—in ways that were both socially fair and efficient. Cooperatives attracted many liberal and left-leaning Americans, yet they had a centrist appeal too. Cooperative housing projects offered a means for ordinary people to bypass political, racial, and ethnic differences to unite toward common social goals.

Henken and his friends were enthusiastic about the cooperative movement and its potential. Many were already involved in consumer cooperatives of some sort, including Henken's brother-in-law Odif Podell, who recalled, "The co-ops always came to solve an economic need.... before the days of the supermarkets, the best buys were in the co-op market."

But it was more than economic benefits that appealed to them. There was also a strong element of idealism—a feeling that cooperative living was not only workable, but also could help create a more just society. Affordable housing, together with green space and cooperative living, would help establish social equity. They were attracted by the possibilities, at least willing to chance the risks, and ready to pay for the privilege. Henken and his friends were not wealthy; most had to struggle to make ends meet. But they believed that if they were willing to work for an alternative way of life, they could make it happen; this influenced their drive to join forces. Against this backdrop David and Priscilla Henken attended an exhibition at the Museum of Modern Art in New York City, an event that would crystallize their beliefs.

USONIA: A NEW AMERICAN SOCIETY

From November 3, 1940, to January 5, 1941, the Museum of Modern Art held a major retrospective of Wright's work. That exhibit offered the truest confirmation that Wright's star had at last risen to preeminence. Wright focused mainly on his recent work, but, most significant, he included a model of Broadacre City, along with manifestoes explaining and expanding on it. Featured prominently were drawings of a planned community in Michigan, which Wright called Usonia 1.

After 1930 Wright spoke more and more often of a quintessentially American community, which he called "Usonia," and a quintessentially American house, which he called "Usonian." He attributed the term "Usonia" to novelist Samuel Butler who, in his utopian novel *Erewhon* ("nowhere" spelled backwards), pitied Americans for having no name of their own. "'The United States' did not appear to him a good title for us as a nation and the word 'American' belonged to us only in common with a dozen or more countries," Wright explained. "So he suggested USONIAN—roots of the word in the word 'unity' or in 'union.' This to me seemed appropriate. So I have often used this word when needing reference to our own country or style." Scholars, however, after searching all of Butler's works, say it is nowhere to be found. Butler's novel was extremely influential in the reformist and utopian debates of the 1910s and 1920s, which may have been why Wright claimed a connection.

The word may also have something to do with a crisis that briefly threatened the acronym U.S.A. In 1910, the Union of South Africa was formed, creating a second U.S.A. Some started to refer to the United States as the U.S.N.A., or United States of North America. Another version was USONA. Wright added an "I" to USONA to get USONIA. The "I" is for euphony—that is, to make the acronym sound better. It also makes it sound more like a country, as in "Utopia." Wright made the word his own for the idealized yet attainable American society that he espoused. In the word "Usonia" one can glimpse many of Wright's utopian aspirations for American architecture, society, and culture.

Wright believed that the ideal American settlement was not the city, which he regarded as overcrowded and unhealthy, but rather the country or suburbs. "You cannot take the country to the city," he admonished in his description of Broadacre City. "The city has to go into the country." He envisioned automobile-owning families living on one-acre plots accessible to goods and services by means of multilane superhighways. This idealized automotive suburb would be largely self-sufficient.

While Wright is often called a "conservative" political thinker, his idiosyncratic political philosophy contained both conservative and liberal elements. In a conservative vein, he distrusted big government and wished to see political power decentralized, entrusted to local settlements as much as possible. In a liberal manner, he was deeply interested in alternative communities, different ways of organizing American togetherness. Throughout the 1940s he designed such communities—government

WRIGHT BELIEVED ARCHITECTURE COULD BE A MEANS OF PERFECTING AMERICAN SOCIETY, A KIND OF MORAL GRAMMAR THAT INCLUDED A HARMONIOUS RELATION BETWEEN DWELLING AND NATURAL SITE, BETWEEN HOUSE AND MATERIALS, AND BETWEEN OUTER AND INNER SPACE.

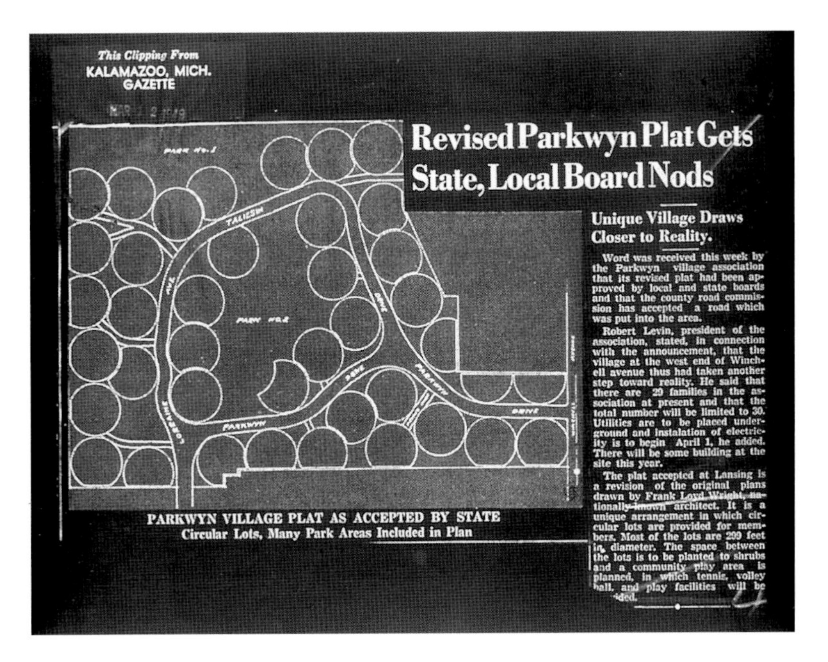

This Clipping From
KALAMAZOO, MICH. GAZETTE

Revised Parkwyn Plat Gets State, Local Board Nods

Unique Village Draws Closer to Reality.

Word was received this week by the Parkwyn village association that its revised plat had been approved by local and state boards and that the county road commission has accepted a road which was put into the area.

Robert Levin, president of the association, stated, in connection with the announcement, that the village at the west end of Winchell avenue thus had taken another step toward reality. He said that there are 29 families in the association at present and that the total number will be limited to 30. Utilities are to be placed underground and instalation of electricity is to begin April 1, he added. There will be some building at the site this year.

The plat accepted at Lansing is a revision of the original plans drawn by Frank Loyd Wright, nationally known architect. It is a unique arrangement in which circular lots are provided for members. Most of the lots are 299 feet in diameter. The space between the lots is to be planted to shrubs and a community play area is planned, in which tennis, volley ball, and play facilities will be provided.

PARKWYN VILLAGE PLAT AS ACCEPTED BY STATE
Circular Lots, Many Park Areas Included in Plan

ARTICLE ABOUT WRIGHT'S PARKWYN VILLAGE, MARCH 1949.

KALAMAZOO, MICHIGAN, GAZETTE

FRANK LLOYD WRIGHT'S USONIA I PROJECT WAS DESCRIBED AT THE MOMA EXHIBIT IN 1940. *COURTESY THE FRANK LLOYD WRIGHT FOUNDATION, SCOTTSDALE, AZ*

housing near Pittsfield, Massachusetts, in 1942, a cooperative homestead venture in Detroit, Michigan, in 1942, Parkwyn Village and Galesburg Country Homes near Kalamazoo, Michigan, in 1947, and other projects in East Lansing, Michigan, and Wheeling, West Virginia—and ran them—as with his own Taliesin, where members learned not only architecture, but also political and moral philosophy. Wright accepted that there was no one right way to organize American communal life, and that any such organization might never be a settled matter, but a dynamic unfolding environment always in progress.

Wright believed architecture could be a means of perfecting American society, a kind of moral grammar that included a harmonious relation between dwelling and natural site, between house and materials, and between outer and inner space. In organic architecture Wright said, "the ground itself predetermines all features; the climate modifies them; available means limit them; function shapes them." Americans (Usonians) could show the world how to build with rather than against nature. Usonians would live in "organically" constructed houses in spiritual harmony within and without. Wright sought to extend the life first mapped out by Ralph Waldo Emerson and Henry David Thoreau—an American life lived with a balance between private and communal life, between home and environment, and between local and central government.

THE TURNING POINT

As David and Priscilla Henken walked through the Museum of Modern Art exhibit viewing the models and drawings of Wright's work, they began to see the means to achieve their dream. Here in Usonia 1 and Broadacre City was a blueprint for a cooperative community that seemed to meld perfectly all of their hopes and desires for a home in the country. Wright wrote, "Any man once square with his own acre or so of ground is sure of a living for himself and his own and sure of some invigorating association with beauty." Organic architecture within an organic community promised a truly American vision, the true enactment of liberty.

Seeing the exhibit was an epiphany for David Henken. He felt that if his dream of a modernist cooperative were ever to materialize, he should give up everything and study architecture with Frank Lloyd Wright. Within the year he wrote to Wright and was accepted into the Taliesin Fellowship at Wright's Spring Green, Wisconsin, home. The tuition was $1100, which also covered room and board, but Priscilla could come along free, Wright told him. Since everyone at the fellowship worked in the kitchen, on the farm, or at the drawing boards, this was not exactly a gift, but it was greatly appreciated.

In 1941 the Henkens closed their apartment, Priscilla obtained a leave of absence from her teaching job, and they joined the fellowship at Taliesin. Working side by side with the forty or so other apprentice architects, they enthusiastically absorbed Wright's philosophy of organic and Usonian architecture. (David would soon give up his engineering work to practice architecture.) While at Taliesin, Henken asked Wright if he would like to help design a cooperative community near New York. Wright enthusiastically agreed to design the site plan and community facilities and to be the consulting architect for the entire project.

HOUSING COOPERATIVES

IN THE UNITED STATES

Joint publication of

Division of Housing Research
HOUSING AND HOME FINANCE AGENCY

Bureau of Labor Statistics
UNITED STATES DEPARTMENT OF LABOR

Housing
Research

DAVID AND PRISCILLA HENKEN NOW HAD A STAR ATTRACTION—FRANK LLOYD WRIGHT—WHEN THEY RETURNED TO NEW YORK IN 1943 WITH THE HOPE OF FOUNDING A COOPERATIVE HOUSING COMMUNITY. THEY BEGAN CALLING THEIR PLAN "THE USONIAN DREAM." "WE WANTED A HOME OF OUR OWN FOR OURSELVES AND THE CHILDREN WE HOPED TO HAVE," PRISCILLA LATER RECALLED, "BUT OUR DESIRE TOOK A PARTICULAR FORM BECAUSE THE IDEAS BEHIND COOPERATIVES AND BROADACRE CITY WERE IN TUNE WITH OUR SOCIAL philosophy and, for David, Mr. Wright's work represented the essence of integrity in architecture."

They began to talk about "Usonia" with an intimate group of family and friends including David's parents, his sister Judeth, and her husband Odif Podell (who would later become mainstays of the group), as well as Priscilla's sister and her husband and four other couples. As Priscilla later recounted, they began to plan in earnest and decided that fifty families would be the cooperative's goal: a number small enough to make a cohesive community yet large enough to share the financial responsibilities. They continued to talk to friends who talked to other friends. "Modern housing was an attractive subject in 1943–44 and any housing was a problem for many young couples, so interest spread as we talked," Priscilla remembered. Soon they were holding meetings every other week in the large Henken apartment. "We poured out the story of the Usonian dream (along with coffee and cake) to hundreds of people. We were even forced to hold several meetings in the larger halls in downtown Manhattan because such crowds wanted to hear about our plans," she added.

Near the end of 1944 a core group of thirteen families agreed to join the effort, a small fraction of the few thousand families that had been either mildly or intensely interested, but had been "discouraged by the war, by high prices, by what seemed like a frightening isolation to the city—bred by the long history of failure in cooperatives and by the near impossibility of securing any financing," Priscilla explained. The Henken apartment became Usonia's de facto headquarters, with a pay phone, filing cabinets, a typewriter, and a mimeograph machine installed in the foyer.

THE COOPERATIVE MOVEMENT PROMISED SOCIAL AND ECONOMIC BENEFITS. *WASHINGTON: DIVISION OF HOUSING RESEARCH, HOUSING AND HOME FINANCE AGENCY AND BUREAU OF LABOR STATISTICS, UNITED STATES DEPARTMENT OF LABOR*

An organizing committee appointed in September 1944 issued a report outlining a plan of action including a membership and financial structure with detailed projections of anticipated expenses. The report noted that its figures were taken from a "Survey of Low-Cost Housing" published in the June 1941 issue of *Architectural Forum.* Many Americans believed that building costs would return to prewar levels, and thus a six-room, 1700-square-foot house was projected to cost $5000. With a twenty-year mortgage (at four and one-half percent interest) monthly expenses including taxes, insurance, heat, and depreciation came to about fifty dollars. The report suggested adding about seven dollars for community expenses and eleven dollars and fourteen cents for commuting to Grand Central Station. The committee believed the estimate to be conservative.

In 1944 members put in $100 each and hired Dorothy Kenyon as their lawyer. Kenyon had a long pedigree as a liberal activist in the cause of civil rights and the cooperative movement. She had been a prominent lawyer for almost three decades in New York City and had served as national director of the American Civil Liberties Union and legal advisor to the New York League of Women Voters. She was active in the American Labor Party and was appointed to a League of Nations committee to study the legal status of women. In January 1939 Kenyon became the first woman judge of the Municipal Court of the City of New York. Kenyon's legal experience, interest in liberal causes, and far-ranging experiences with organizational, philosophical, and legal aspects of cooperative communities made her a likely advisor.

A ROCHDALE COOPERATIVE

From its beginning in 1944 Usonia was planned as a Rochdale-style cooperative of about fifty members. Rochdale Cooperative, Inc. was one of the biggest American cooperative societies. It derived its principles from the Rochdale Equitable Pioneers Society, a group of underemployed weavers in nineteenth-century England who banded together for mutual benefit during the exploitative years of the Industrial Revolution. A signal feature of the Rochdale-style cooperative was that all members needed to take on individual and communal risk to realize mutual benefit. The theory was that out of mutual risk a mutuality of purpose would emerge. People would actually come to have a stake in each other's lives, a stake that supposedly would transcend the interest represented by the money.

Usonia's goal was to build such a community of individually designed, cooperatively owned, affordable homes on at least one-acre sites in a suburb of New York City with the guidance and participation of Frank Lloyd Wright. Members were accepted after a compatibility and financial-screening process. After the co-op found suitable property and Wright developed a site plan, the accepted member would select a site and an approved architect to design a new home. The homes were to be built and owned by the cooperative, while the member received a ninety-nine-year renewable lease on the home and site.

Once accepted, a member of Usonia Homes paid a membership fee of $100 and purchased one $5 share of the cooperative. Each family was expected to contribute $50 each month toward their own building account until they reached forty percent of the expected cost of their house plus a sum allocated for the site, architectural ser-

FUNDAMENTALS
of
Consumer Cooperation

NINTH EDITION by V. S. ALANNE

A thoro discussion of the theory and practical application of principles of consumer cooperation by an author who has pioneered in teaching Cooperation in America.

COOPERATIVE PUBLISHING ASSOCIATION
SUPERIOR, WISCONSIN

left: CONSUMER CO-OPS, AS WELL AS GOVERNMENT PUBLICATIONS, INFORMED USONIANS IN THE CREATION AND OPERATION OF THEIR COMMUNITY. *SUPERIOR, WISCONSIN: COOPERATIVE PUBLISHING ASSOCIATION*

right: COVER OF FIRST USONIA BROCHURE, 1946.
COLLECTION ROLAND REISLEY

"WE WERE LIVING IN MANHATTAN IN A COOPERATIVE APARTMENT. WE CARED ABOUT CO-OPS....WE BELONGED TO FOOD CO-OPS....USONIA WAS TO BE A TRUE ROCHDALE COOPERATIVE....ONE MEMBER, ONE VOTE REGARDLESS OF RACE, RELIGION, CREED."

vices, and other fees. Forty percent was believed to be enough of a down payment to make it easier to obtain a mortgage for the rest. The money was placed into a joint fund in the name of the cooperative but credited to an individual account in the member family's name. Members joining later would have to catch up with their earlier counterparts.

Having agreed on their goal and structure, the founders and early members incorporated under the laws of the State of New York as a Rochdale Cooperative in 1945. In their now-official title, Usonia Homes: A Cooperative Inc., they paid homage to the legacy of Usonian houses Wright had designed during the previous decade. On January 28, 1945, at the first formal membership meeting, the group adopted a set of by-laws that called for the election of a board of five directors, who in turn would elect officers of the corporation. The organization had an ambitious agenda. It needed to enroll members, raise money, plan financially, locate and acquire land, develop roads and utilities, make arrangements with architects, and then build the houses. This was quite a challenge for a very young group with limited means and virtually no experience. But they were optimistic that working together they could accomplish it.

COOPERATIVE IDEALISM

At the onset of the twenty-first century it may be difficult to appreciate the appeal of the consumer cooperative of the 1940s. Despite considerable acceptance of co-ops in Europe during the nineteenth century, in the United States, with its individualistic society and sense of limitless expansion, there was not much cooperative activity until early in the twentieth century, and that primarily among farming and industrial associations. The growth of consumer cooperatives and the somewhat analogous labor unions soon followed.

While cooperatives (including Usonia) attracted many liberal and left-wing Americans, for a time social experimentation was in the mainstream, even governmentally encouraged. In 1934 the Bureau of Labor Statistics prepared Bulletin 608 dealing with the organization and management of consumer co-ops, cooperative petroleum, and cooperative housing efforts. Even the U.S. Senate's General Housing Act of 1945 included a provision for low-interest Federal Housing Administration mortgages for a "nonprofit mutual ownership housing corporation" restricted to members "of such corporation."

In February 1946, as interest in co-ops increased, Bulletin 608 was revised as Bulletin 858 to bring the subject up to "present practice." In the "letter of transmittal," the authors noted that they wished "especially to acknowledge the valuable contributions and suggestions of Dale Johnson... [and] Dorothy Kenyon." Johnson was an active figure in the cooperative housing movement. Among many other things, Kenyon, Usonia's legal counsel, was the Eastern Cooperative League's lawyer. Bulletins 608 and 858 put forward a philosophy and principles that precisely matched the views of many early Usonians. Adherents often had a quasi-religious scrupulosity, demanding strict observance and purity of principle. As members of the Eastern Cooperative League, Usonians received the *Cooperator* magazine.

Usonians were rank-and-file or board members of more than twenty cooperative groups. "We were living in Manhattan in a cooperative apartment," recalled Usonia resident Fay Watts. "We cared about co-ops... we belonged to food co-ops. We also believed in interracial living.... Usonia was to be a true Rochdale cooperative.... One member, one vote regardless of race, religion, creed." Members joined the Usonia cooperative with the understanding that they took on certain responsibilities and duties toward the community as well as communal risk, and that voluntary service was its strength. In the ensuing formative years, before they had land, financing, or enough members, communications to Usonians were often addressed to "cooperators" and almost invariably signed "cooperatively yours."

The early Usonians hammered out the shape of their cooperative in an astonishing number of meetings at the Henken apartment, the Labor Temple on 14th Street, and the Cooperative Cafeteria on 25th Street. The Usonians' membership meetings, board meetings, and even dinners, parties, and happy hours were characterized by vigorous, often loud debate on organic architecture, social theory, and aesthetics. Early meetings were especially strenuous. "Those were the best of the arguments," one Usonian remembered. "They were loud, they were endless, they sometimes were pointless, and I can't say nobody's feelings got hurt. But they were invigorating, and everybody took part."

The cooperative established several committees to address Usonia's needs: first finance, membership, building, and publicity; next administrative, education, social, and technical; finally land, newsletter, and historical. Members were expected to participate actively in committees. Despite the co-op's representative structure of elected officers, directors, by-laws, architectural leaders, and committee chairs, Usonia became a direct, sometimes chaotic democracy. Every member wanted to hear and be heard about every issue. Perhaps this occurred because of members' longtime experience with clubs, unions, and co-ops, or possibly because of the enormity of the financial investment and the sense of a lifetime family commitment that fueled the debate. Though there was an unanimity on major goals, there was frequent division on how to achieve them.

ENROLLING NEW MEMBERS

Attracting prospects to Usonia was probably the least difficult challenge. Publicizing the planned community by word of mouth, through organizations, unions, clubs, co-ops, and the press took leg work, but interest in new homes was high, and many people were curious to hear about cooperatively built, affordable, Frank Lloyd Wright-supervised homes. The March 1946 *Newsonian* newsletter reported a meeting with 75 prospects at the Cooperative Cafeteria in New York, and described some of their questions: What happens to a septic tank if you have weekend guests? If there is no cellar, where do children play when it rains? What about movies, restaurants, civilization? What if there is a commuter train wreck? The city folk had much to learn about life in exurbia. In May another 100 people met; in August 200 more.

An early "fact sheet" described the community's goals: "How are we a cooperative? In that we are pooling our financial resources and initiative to plan and build a community of modern homes with advantages we could not obtain individually." Those homes "will be organic in design" and "will grow out of and reflect: a) the materials employed; b) the technique of the times; c) the site chosen; d) the needs and personalities of the occupants; e) the creative personality of the architects." One can hear the echoes of Wright in such passages as "no two homes will be alike" and "wherever function is considered, the occupant will be regarded as a human being and not as a machine."

A brochure was written to define further these goals. The first edition, dated May 1945, said the cost of a home would be about $5000 including land and basic built-in furniture. (Five-thousand dollars was not entirely unrealistic for a low-cost house at the time; developers offered homes for even less, but of course the Usonian house was to be of superior quality.) An early cover of the brochure featured Wright's Fallingwater; a later edition showed several of Wright's Usonian houses; and the 1950 brochure published the new Watts House in Usonia. The brochure thus emphasized the prestige of consulting architect Frank Lloyd Wright, who was described therein as "perhaps the most distinguished architect in the world." It did not imply that Wright himself would design all of the houses. Rather, it explained, "He will plan the community as a whole, design the community buildings, approve the design of each individual home, and design some individual homes himself. Members may choose the architects for their own homes from a group of architects approved by Wright." For those who wanted to learn more, the membership committee scheduled meetings with small groups.

Applicants for membership had to fill out a financial questionnaire and submit an elaborate application with questions on political tolerance, race and religion, literary tastes, family, educational and vocational background, hobbies, sports, finances, and personal "cooperativeness." (The application amuses Usonians today, but was the earnest effort of two young psychologist members.) The procedure for reviewing applications was subjective, as described by Priscilla Henken in an April 1946 letter to a Detroit, Michigan, cooperative housing group. "As for qualifications for membership, choosing people is at best a highly subjective task. We have a membership committee of six (a representative cross-section of group opinion, we hope), whose job it is to meet all prospective applicants several times.... At [the] last meeting, the couple is met alone. Then the committee votes on acceptance or rejection, and the recommendation is submitted to the Board of Directors for a final decision. I repeat that this is subjective, no matter how highly objective we may try to be. The questionnaire... gives some indication as to likes and dislikes, prejudices, interests, hobbies, and general ability to communicate sympathetically with present members of the group. However, we don't expect or want any definite set of answers."

During the planning years there were indeed rejections, some bitterly protested. One applicant complained to the Eastern Cooperative League, which was then processing Usonia's petition for membership. A league representative immediately challenged Usonia, asserting that membership must be open to anyone who

EARLY APPLICATION SOUGHT TO IDENTIFY COMMITTED, COMPATIBLE MEMBERS. *COLLECTION ROLAND REISLEY*

Check whether you would like, dislike, or be indifferent to each of the following characteristics in your neighbors. Mark L if you would like such a characteristic in a neighbor, D if you would dislike it, and I if it would not matter.

Active musician	____	Aggressiveness	____	Agnostic	____
Anarchist	____	Atheist	____	Catholic	____
Chicken raiser	____	Chinese	____	Christian Scientist	____
Communist	____	Democrat	____	Devoutly religious	____
Dog or cat owner	____	Fascist	____	Fundamentalist	____
Hindu	____	Irish	____	Italian	____
Japanese	____	Jew	____	Liberal	____
Mixed marriage	____	Negro	____	Pacifist	____
Protestant	____	Reactionary	____	Republican	____
Retiring	____	Socialist	____	Sloppy housekeeper	____
Trotskyite	____				

Would you object to living with people falling into any of the categories which you disliked in the preceding question? ____________________

Which categories: ____

____

Check which of the following community functions you would consider essential and which luxuries. Mark E for essential and L for luxury. Answer from the standpoint of community rather than your personal needs.

After-school play group	____	Amateur theatre group	____
Apiary (beehives)	____	Bowling alley	____
Community center	____	Dances	____
Glee club or chorus	____	Greenhouse	____
Grocery or shopping service	____	Group health service	____
Gymnasium	____	Horse-back riding	____
Laundry	____	Lectures	____
Library	____	Livestock raising	____
Maid service	____	Maintenance	____
Movies	____	Nursery school	____
Orchestra	____	Playing fields or courts	____
Ski trail	____	Swimming pool	____
Tennis court	____	Truck garden	____
Work shop	____	Others ____________	

Check whether you attend each of the following functions frequently, occasionally, or never. Mark F if frequently, O if occasionally, and N if never.

Art exhibits	____	Ball games	____	Ballets	____
Concerts	____	Dance recitals	____	Lectures	____
Movies	____	Museums	____	Plays	____
Others ____________		____________		____________	

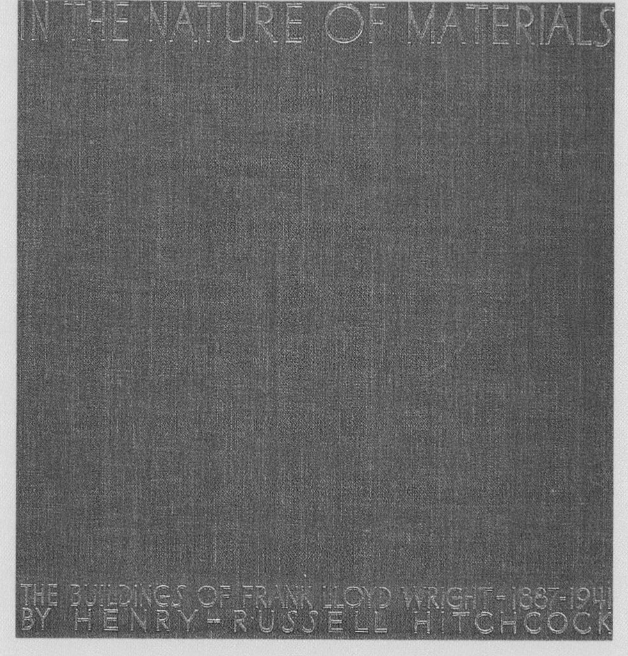

USONIA'S LIBRARY HELPED MEMBERS LEARN TO SELECT AND WORK WITH ARCHITECTS.

clockwise from left:

NEW YORK: SIMON AND SCHUSTER, 1945

NEW YORK: DUELL, SLOAN AND PEARCE, 1941

NEW YORK: DUELL, SLOAN AND PEARCE, 1942

agreed to its principles. Usonia's explanation—in part, that it hoped to exclude any political activity—was accepted. (In the mid-1940s many left-liberal and socialist progressives were vigilantly anticommunistic and suspicious of infiltration by those whom they thought may have had communist leanings.) In those early applications, the most frequently stated characteristics of a neighbor that would be objectionable were "fascist" and "reactionary." But "chicken raiser" and "sloppy housekeeper" were also often mentioned. (Decades later committee members guessed that some of the "probably not compatible" applicants might have turned out just fine.)

The membership committee tried diligently to assemble a compatible group that was committed to Usonia's cooperative and architectural principles. Of the original forty-seven families who settled in Usonia, thirty underwent this interviewing process. In later years, however, when the unforeseen high building costs and growing financial difficulties prompted the urgency to attract new members, the focus of membership interviews changed, shifting from requiring commitment to the architectural and sociological views to their acceptance, and essentially determining interest in being part of the cooperative.

UNDERSTANDING "ORGANIC" ARCHITECTURE

Clearly the members wanted "modern" homes, but most were not aware of the differences between Wright's "organic" architecture and the International Bauhaus style, or simply "contemporary" buildings. In the 1940s, before the postwar exodus to the suburbs, these young members—most in their twenties or thirties, living in urban apartments, and perhaps never having lived in their own houses—were now to choose an architect, define their needs, and reconcile them with the anticipated cost. Educational activities were designed to address this, but it was not expected that all members would reach a serious understanding of architectural style. The architectural character of the community would be assured by Frank Lloyd Wright's approval of all architects and their designs. Most early Usonians found great appeal in Wright's concept of modern "organic" architecture. The open floor plans, walls of windows that opened easily to the outside, natural materials, and integrated furnishings of his Usonian house were key attractions. Most of the houses also had broad, flat roofs with deep overhangs that gave them a reassuring sense of shelter. Standardized materials, a carport instead of a garage, and a modular design kept costs low. These innovative designs were simple yet elegant, and excited the young Usonians anxious to move ahead from the past.

To help Usonians learn how to define their needs for a new home and how to select the right architect, the education committee, along with Usonia's librarian member Julia Brody, outlined a suggested reading list which included: *In the Nature of Materials* and *On Architecture* by Frank Lloyd Wright; *If You Want to Build a House* by Elizabeth Mock; *Good-bye, Mr. Chippendale* by T. H. Robsjohn-Gibbings; *Tomorrow's House* by George Nelson and Henry Wright; *The Book of Houses* by Simon Breines and John P. Dean; and *Organization and Management of Cooperative Mutual Housing Associations, Bulletin No. 858* from the U.S. Department of Labor—as well as twenty additional titles and architectural journals.

During the years 1945 through 1947 the committee also organized meetings, lectures, and field trips. There were repeated visits to the Wright-designed Ben Raebuhn

House on Long Island, to the Museum of Modern Art where the model of a proposed Wright-designed house for Gerald Loeb was on display, and to Wright's Plaza Hotel suite to view a model of the Guggenheim Museum. Wright visited with members in March 1947; Wright apprentices Edgar Kaufmann, Jr. (whose father built Fallingwater) and Edgar Tafel also paid visits in early 1947. Architects Charles Abrams and Simon Breines also met with the group.

THE FINANCIAL PLAN—RAISING THE MONEY

While Usonians educated themselves about architecture, they necessarily also studied economic planning. Knowing that a cooperative of modern houses could not easily obtain financing or assure prospective members' financial security, the founding members were determined to develop and communicate a sound fiscal plan. Financially oriented members presented to the co-op detailed analyses on which the minimum investment of forty percent prior to construction was based. Building cost estimates were based on the June 1941 *Architectural Forum* "Survey of Low Cost Housing," which reported on $3000 to $6000 houses (of four to seven rooms) with total monthly costs of thirty to sixty dollars. These costs—based on convection heating, rather than the newer radiant heating, and a twenty percent cash down payment—were thought to be slightly higher than the planned Usonians.

The estimated cost of a typical house, however, was rising as indicated in successive editions of the Usonia brochure: January 1946, $5–7500; September 1946, $8500; September 1947, $8500–16,000; Spring 1948, $15–30,000; Spring 1950, $20,000–up. Many early members' incomes did not increase as fast as building costs, and a number of them had to withdraw from the cooperative.

LAND

Dorothy Kenyon, a strong supporter of the cooperative movement and Usonia's lawyer, was generously committed to its success—almost as a mentor. In 1945, shortly after incorporation, she advised Usonia that it might be able to buy land in the country inexpensively at a tax foreclosure auction. She was an acquaintance of Ed Cox, Attorney of the Town of Mount Pleasant in Westchester County, New York, and learned from him that several suitable parcels were subject to such sale.

Usonia was able to secure an option to acquire three contiguous parcels, about eighty-six acres, for $19,000—approximately the amount of the taxes that had not been paid since the 1920s—if, when auctioned, no higher bid was received. Though Cox's experience and some promised "legerdemain" at the auction suggested high confidence in the outcome, the auction had to be public and some uncertainty necessarily persisted. To minimize the possibility of competitive bids, Usonia's board of directors was advised not to disclose widely the land proceedings. The irresolution caused some resentment and loss of prospective members, yet it was generally thought to be a fait accompli.

Usonians considered other land in Long Island, New Jersey, and Westchester County, but not very seriously, because for most of them the property in Mount Pleasant seemed ideal. David Henken recalled, "I fell in love with the land. It had the rolling quality of Taliesin in Wisconsin: rocky knolls, clumps of trees, springs, and a brook or two. The hills and valleys would provide dramatic settings and a sense of privacy." Priscilla Henken, in her essay "A Broadacre Project," described it this way: "Surrounded on three sides by a pine-tree watershed that forms a permanent green belt, it is hilly, rolling, with pleasant little brooks, fine old trees as well as much new growth, stone fences which are remnants of ancient farms." A beautiful tract of woods and hills, the land was protected east and south by the huge Kensico watershed and on the west by the 135-acre Mastick estate and Bard's working farm—his cows also grazed on "Usonia's" land. Nearby, the suburban hamlets of Thornwood and Chappaqua and the somewhat larger Village of Pleasantville had developed around railroad stations. A little farther away large tracts of land remained undeveloped. (Today, more than fifty years later, there is acre-lot development all around, giving the area the look of suburbia, but Usonia remains a wooded rural enclave.)

In their enthusiasm Usonians organized weekend picnics and visits to the land. Not many members had automobiles in 1945 and 1946, so they came by train—New York Central from Grand Central Station to Thornwood—and then walked uphill about two miles. To the mostly city born and bred Usonians, accustomed to public transportation and walking to schools and stores, this really was the "country." Even though the land was not yet Usonia's, the community agreed that some fire-fighting equipment would be needed and that the opportunity to purchase "war surplus" bargains should not be ignored. A water tank and pump mounted on a trailer was acquired in July 1946, towed up to Mount Pleasant, and stored near the land.

In March 1946 an additional eleven-acre parcel, north and adjacent to the original three parcels, was being processed by Mount Pleasant for sale at the same time for an estimated $3–4000. There was considerable debate on whether to seek it. The majority of the board of directors, however, felt that the expense was minimal, interest of the membership was great, and the property's connection to Bear Ridge Road desirable. Perhaps most significant, the town attorney indicated that with an agreed buyer the auction would get little publicity, while without a buyer the sale would be publicized, with the possibility of attracting other bidders and raising the cost for the optioned parcels. The effort to acquire the land was anxiously monitored and regularly reported to the board and members. Because of unforeseen delays, two years would pass before the auction took place.

MORE DEBATE, MORE COOPERATION

Usonians enjoyed social activities together in the city and at the "land." But since they could not build anything, there was plenty of time for debate and argument. The intensive debates during 1945 and 1946 are richly documented in the community's correspondence, communications, minutes of meetings, and newsletters. Usonia's goal was to build houses, but until they had enough members, money, and the land, they focused their energies on developing the organization. To help orchestrate discussions, a procedural policy required that "the copy of Roberts' *Rules Of Order* must be present at each board and membership meeting" and an article from *Cooperator* magazine, "Order In The House," on how to hold efficient meetings without bogging down on side issues and arguments was distributed to the membership. Clearly, cooperation was debatable. The board of directors and committees complained of miscommunication and undefined authority. One director observed that "the more committees we create, the more time we spend discussing their operation."

Soon the board was meeting every week, sometimes twice a week, often with other members attending.

A 1946 *NEWSONIAN* REMINDED MEMBERS THAT "OUR ARCHITECTURE WILL BE USONIAN OR ORGANIC, NOT MODERN OR FUNCTIONAL, WHICH BRINGS TO MIND THE STARK BARREN CUBES OF THE BAUHAUS. USONIAN ARCHITECTURE ADAPTS TO NATURE AND THE INDIVIDUAL."

(Being a director was not easy. The long, often contentious meetings sometimes provoked resignations. At times, joining the board was just a matter of being willing to serve on it.) Some committees were also very active in gathering information on water systems, sewage disposal, central heating, and the possibility of Usonia generating its own electricity. Besides the core issues of creating a cooperative, attracting members, educating members, and financing the project, there were related philosophical and policy issues. Proposals to organize and reorganize were regularly discussed. A majority of members might not agree with a board majority. Nevertheless, a foundation and principles that would shape the future community and its membership emerged from the energetic idealistic ferment.

One primary principle was architecture. A 1946 *Newsonian* reminded members that "our architecture will be Usonian or organic, not modern or functional, which brings to mind the stark barren cubes of the Bauhaus. Usonian architecture adapts to nature and the individual." Another principle involved essentials versus luxuries. Determined that a majority not impose nonessential expenses, members were asked their opinion of sixty-seven items. Most essential were water systems, roads, and fire-fighting equipment, and least essential were an apiary, golf course, and stable. Many of the items were quite unrealistic, but the principle was established that members would not be obliged to pay for luxuries. Instead, if a group of members wanted a facility, a sub-co-op could be approved. In later years the children's play group, swimming pool, and tennis courts were formed in this way.

A third principle addressed risks and commitment. The intense commitment of the early Usonians to their core values, ideals, and each other while facing the risks of radical design, the cooperative structure, uncertain costs, distance from the city, and the skepticism of their more experienced parents and financial advisers was attractive to people who wanted to join Usonia.

David Henken—the group's founder, teacher, guiding figure, liaison with Frank Lloyd Wright, and vigorous exponent of cooperative ideals—equipped the "office" (really the living room in the apartment he and his wife shared with his sister and brother-in-law) with drawing boards and reference materials and engaged in prodigious correspondence, gathering information on materials, construction, landscape, building equipment, and, of course, acceptable architects. Soon he was joined in the office by Aaron Resnick, a civil engineer and structural designer who had recently become a member and would become a significant architect and engineer in Usonia.

Henken also corresponded with other members of cooperative associations, particularly with Dale

Johnson, the housing consultant of the Eastern Cooperative League (ECL). With access to World War II surplus stocks and mass purchasing power, ECL could, presumably, offer building materials advantageously to housing co-ops. Johnson scrutinized Usonia's application for membership for true adherence to cooperative principles. Ultimately satisfied, an active relationship ensued. (Until 1953 Usonia was represented at ECL conventions and committees by Aaron Resnick, Ralph Miller, Herb Brandon, Odif Podell, and others, and David Henken became secretary of the executive board of the ECL Housing Service Project.)

Thus, in less than five years, Usonians had envisioned a community, incorporated as a cooperative, retained Kenyon as their lawyer and Wright as their chief architect, attracted a large number of interested people, and begun to amass a joint fund that would help see Usonia Homes through some extremely difficult times ahead. This group of dreamers was in search of affordable houses in the country and a community full of real neighbors with whom they shared more than a fence. Circumstances would pare down the numbers to the extremely committed, the ones who enjoyed calling themselves "the die-hards." Two years had passed since obtaining the option on land in Mount Pleasant. All that remained, it seemed, was the auction at which they hoped to acquire the land—and then actual building could commence.

Chapter Three BUILDING USONIA

THE MONTHLY

NEWSONIAN

ALL THE NEWS THAT FITS WE PRINT

BUBLISHED BY USONIA HOMES, A COOPERATIVE, INC.

page 1 SAVE THIS ISSUE January, 1947

LAND! LAND! LAND!

U S O N I A A C Q U I R E S L O N G - S O U G H T A C R E A G E

ACTUAL AUCTION ALLEVIATES ANTICIPATION ANGUISH

On January 21st we took title to our land. From now on we can really call it ours. After all the postponments and obstacles, we managed to get for a sum that we had hardly dared believe possible. For quite a time and right up to the auction it looked as though we were going to have to pay through the nose, but like all fairy stories this event in our development had a happy ending.

On a bleak stormy morning in mid-December, our Board along with Judge Kenyon boarded the early train for White Plains. Faces were long, eyes were crusty, we were warned that there would be a lot of competition at the bidding, members had to pretend that they didn't know one another and weren't going up as a group for even the walls of railroad cars have ears.

However, the miserable weather was an ally in disguise as it discouraged competition, especially you-know-who. We were very fortunate in having a man of the calibre of Judge Kenyon's associate to handle the bidding.

After the auction was over the faces of the Board had changed quite a bit. The impossible had happened. Priscilla Henken was called and she in turn phoned every member of Usonia to carry the good news from White Plains to Brooklyn.

To the Editor:

We were so excited to hear that "our land" had become our land, that we gave way to the overpowering impulse and drove up there. The "we", besides being editorial, included the Bleifelds and the L. Resnicks.

It was a crisp blowy day and the sun glinted bravely over the rippled surface of the reservoir as we approached the side road. Instead of turning in we continued around the bend, and followed the road that skirts the northern part of the property. (We seem to be protected by a sturdy cyclone fence for the greater part of the land which adjoins the road.) The abandoned school house looked neat and trim in gray and white as we passed. We also noticed several homes - estates even - directly across from the

(cont'd on page 3)

"LAND! LAND! LAND!" PROCLAIMED THE JANUARY 1947 *NEWSONIAN*, USONIA'S OFFICIAL NEWSLETTER. THE DREAM OF OWNING THE PERFECT STRETCH OF LAND WAS AT LAST WITHIN REACH. BENEATH THE HEADLINE, "ACTUAL AUCTION ALLEVIATES ANTICIPATION ANGUISH," THE CO-OP'S PLAN TO ACQUIRE THE COVETED PROPERTY IN WESTCHESTER COUNTY, NEW YORK, UNFOLDED: "ON A BLEAK STORMY MORNING IN MID-DECEMBER OUR BOARD, ALONG WITH JUDGE KENYON, BOARDED THE EARLY TRAIN FOR WHITE PLAINS. FACES WERE long, eyes were crusty. We were warned that there would be competition at the bidding. Members had to pretend that they weren't going up as a group, for even the walls of railroad cars have ears. However, the miserable weather was an ally in disguise as it discouraged competition and we were very fortunate in having Judge Kenyon's associate to handle the bidding."

After the auction faces changed quite a bit. The improbable had happened. Usonia had been successful in its bid, paying $23,000 for the ninety-seven acres. "We took title to the land," the article enthused. "We can really call it ours. After all the postponements and obstacles, we got it for a sum that we had hardly dared believe possible. But like fairy stories, this event in our development had a happy ending."

ENTER FRANK LLOYD WRIGHT

Now that Usonia Homes had a site, it was time to prepare a topographical survey and send it to Frank Lloyd Wright together with a statement of requirements for the design of the community. In September 1945, David Henken visited Taliesin with news of Usonia's progress. Shortly thereafter Wright spoke to the Usonia board of directors and members at his apartment in New York as one of several talks Wright gave the group on organic architecture and related philosophical ideas. Such appearances were convenient for Wright: he kept an apartment at the Plaza Hotel in New York and was frequently in town for his work on the Guggenheim Museum. Wright evinced enthusiasm about the future of the community in several interviews of the time.

NEWSONIAN DESCRIBES LONG-AWAITED PURCHASE OF THE LAND.

COLLECTION ROLAND REISLEY

Wright's previously understood agreement to be Usonia's chief designer and supervising architect was formalized with a contract in January 1946. Early in March 1947, Wright accompanied Henken and Usonians John Troll (then chairman of the board), Aaron Resnick, Bernard Kessler, and deBlois Bush to see the site. Wright said he thought it was "beautiful and ideal for our project, but remember that it would be quite easy to spoil it with bad housing." He also complimented those responsible for picking the site. An account of the visit in the *Newsonian* added, "Naturally Mr. Wright's comments were not limited to Usonia alone. He gave his ideas on New York City architecture, American architecture, highway design, bridge design, plans for the United Nations, Russian architecture, French architecture, his own place in history, sycamore trees, pine trees, rock formations, Taliesin, formal education, and many other things. All were amazed at the vitality of this man's mind and none will forget the experience for a long time. Mr. Wright promised to speak to us again in May."

Henken personally delivered the topographic map and requirements to Wright. During the visit, Henken confirmed an earlier agreement that Wright would design five homes—but not more—for individual members. Wright, Henken noted later, "stressed the importance of having the client make his own decision as to the architect he uses" and voiced his concern that materials be used "properly." Wright said he would visit and speak with members in June and try to bring drawings with him, and that he expected separate payment for the site plan.

Several months later, Wright presented his drawing for the site plan. The drawings evinced Wright's work of the late 1940s, when his interest in the circle as a geometric basis of design was approaching its peak. In Usonia's site plan, he laid out each building lot as a circle of about one acre. Wright explained that the circles, touching only tangentially rather than "cheek by jowl," as in conventional suburban subdivisions, would result in greater individual privacy and a sense of much greater space. The wedge-shaped areas in between the circles would be reserved as buffers of green. In some areas, a group of six circles would enclose another circle that could serve as a communal park. There were to be no fences or other site boundary delineations (a prohibition that Usonia has retained to the present) and sites were chosen to make the most of both solar exposure and shade. A network of narrow, serpentine roads connected the sites and meandered naturally with the topography of the countryside. In all respects it was a Wrightian performance, a design for a modern, organic community integrated with open, natural space. The plan was received enthusiastically and, when published, generated wide interest and curiosity.

Despite its obvious brilliance, Wright's initial drawings did not respond to all of Usonia's requirements. Henken responded to Wright along with a list of community requirements and a list of sites that for one reason or another—northern slope, draining difficulties, impossibility of terrain—were undesirable. Today, knowing the profound financial difficulties the community would soon face, it is difficult to comprehend the lofty aspirations Henken outlined to Wright:

"We're contemplating the purchase of additional land that would allow the vineyards to be shifted closer to the orchard.... We note the lack of a nursery, playing fields, tennis courts, and special hobby facilities in the community center, as well as a store or shopping service facility. . . . In the community building we feel the lounge portion could readily be absorbed in the recreation and alcove portion and that the space thus saved might be utilized for store, office, and hobby facilities. . . . Could you proceed with the necessary changes, as well as make suggestions for the nursery and children's playground?"

The early Usonians—all apartment dwellers accustomed to city conveniences—clearly thought of their land in northern Westchester County as quite isolated and remote. They apparently did not realize that many of these amenities were already developing in the suburbs and that some of their requests would be unnecessary. Wright did not redraw the site plan, but did send preliminary drawings for a community center. It was not built; there was never enough money for it.

In the ensuing months, however, closer study of the topography and discussions with Wright led to some revisions in the site plan. Recreational and children's play areas were designated, the diameter of each site circle was increased from 200 to 217.5 feet (a "builder's acre" in Mount Pleasant) and their locations shifted slightly to better accommodate the roads. The revised plan, drawn by Henken and Resnick, was sent to Wright in November, along with a letter requesting an appointment for them to bring some preliminary house drawings to Taliesin for approval. A few days later Wright replied:

> Dear David:
>
> I approve the changes in the site-plan as previously discussed with me in N.Y. and now made by your committee. The site-plan services are now rendered and enclosed is a bill for that service. In the two Michigan plans [for Galesburg Country Homes and Parkwyn Village], one 21 houses, the other 40, we charged a fee of $1500.00, agreeing to charge it off pro rata as the houses were built as all were to be built by myself. In your larger scheme for 55 houses only 5 of which I build I think a fee of $2000.00 for the site-plan reasonable in the circumstances. You have sent us $500.00. We are therefore sending a bill for $1500.00. We leave early this year for Arizona. You would better come out next week as convenient to you.
>
> My best to you all—especially Priscilla and the babe
>
> Frank Lloyd Wright, November 8th, 1947

Well before receiving even the preliminary site plan, the co-op held numerous discussions about the best method for site selection. With a goal of fifty paid-up members, the group expected conflicting site choices. To minimize these conflicts, the co-op developed a "Site Request Form" along with an arbitration procedure. A number of members thought the plan was unnecessarily complicated and noted that it had changed with changing membership of the board of directors. A simplified method was then adopted that resulted in most members receiving the site that they had requested. By early fall 1947, thirty sites had been assigned. Twenty-two of them were first choices.

THE DESIGN PANEL

The cooperative regarded Wright's ideas as key to the design of the community. At its earliest formal meeting in 1945, Usonia assigned the responsibility of maintaining the relationship with Wright and implementing his design to a building committee comprised of Usonia founder David Henken and Bernard Kessler, who was an engineer and architect. The board formalized this assignment with a personal contract with Henken.

THE MONTHLY

NEWSONIAN

ALL THE NEWS THAT FITS WE PRINT

PUBLISHED BY USONIA HOMES, A COOPERATIVE, INC.

page 1 SAVE THIS ISSUE March, 1947

FRANK LLOYD WRIGHT VISITS USONIA

ENTHUSIASTIC ON CHOICE OF LAND

3/11/47 Our Building Committee met Frank L. Wright at the Hotel Plaza early in the morning and drove out to the land. Mr. Wright was most enthusiastic about all aspects of the property and expressed the hope that we do nothing to spoil it. The Building Committee assured him that it was to prevent any misuse that we had asked him to be the supervising architect.

While Mr. Wright could not do any definite planning since he has not received the topographical map (which will be very soon) he did make many general suggestions to the committee on just how such terrain should be handled and began turning over in his mind ideas about the community center.

Among many things, Mr. Wright suggested that members choose their own architects that no rigid standardization be imposed to limit the architects and recommended some of his ex-apprentices who he felt would be fully qualified to design Usonian houses.

Naturally Mr. Wright's comments were not limited to Usonia alone. He gave his ideas on N.Y.C. architecture, American architecture, highway design, bridge design, plans for the U.N., Russian architecture, French Architecture, his own place in history, sycamore trees, pine trees, rock formations, Taliesin, formal education and many other things.

All were amazed at the vitality and originality of this man's mind. None will forget the experience for a long time. They realized they were in the presence of real genius.

Everyone will have the chance to meet Mr. Wright for he has promised to speak to us in May.

NEW MEMBERS

Herbert and Ada Brandon
3115 Ave. I, Brooklyn, New York
Cl 8-2151

Herbert is an advertising manager and Ada takes care of Carl who is 2½ years old. They have both traveled a good deal Cuba, Haiti, South America, Panama, Honduras etc. Herb likes to spend his leisure time playing chess, checkers, writing, playing cards, in photography, reading discussing politics with others,

They both read a great many magazines and periodicals. Ada is interested in arts and crafts, dramatics, piano, painting, and drawing, shop work, gardening, reading, sculpture, singing, dancing, costume design and theatrical arts.

* * * * * * * * * * * * * * *

Sidney & Florence Benzer
111-50 76th Road, Forest Hills, N.Y.
Bo 3-1135

Sidney is a dentist and Florence is an assistant art director for a publication. They both attend art exhibits, concerts and museums frequently. Sidney is interested in arts and crafts, horticulture, shop work, gardening, orchestra, photography, reading also birding and tropical fish collecting. Florence shares his interest with the addition of painting and drawing. She makes some of the loveliest jewelry and handbags we have ever seen. Nothing amateur about them, strictly professional. They both enjoy boating, tennis, hiking, swimming and pingpong.

EDUCATIONAL SOCIAL

Edgar Taffel, one of the recommended architects, will speak on March 21st at the Blue Ribbon Restaurant, 145 W. 44 St. Time - 8:30, Refreshments, Information on Building Committee and Architects.

Price 50¢ each

left: FRANK LLOYD WRIGHT VIEWING THE SITE PLAN WITH AARON RESNICK (LEFT) AND DAVID HENKEN (RIGHT), THE MEMBER/ARCHITECTS WHO WERE DIRECTING CONSTRUCTION OF ROADS, WATER SYSTEM, AND ELECTRICITY LINES. *© PEDRO E. GUERRERO*

right: *NEWSONIAN*, MARCH 1947, DESCRIBES EARLIER WRIGHT VISIT TO THE LAND. *COLLECTION ROLAND REISLEY*

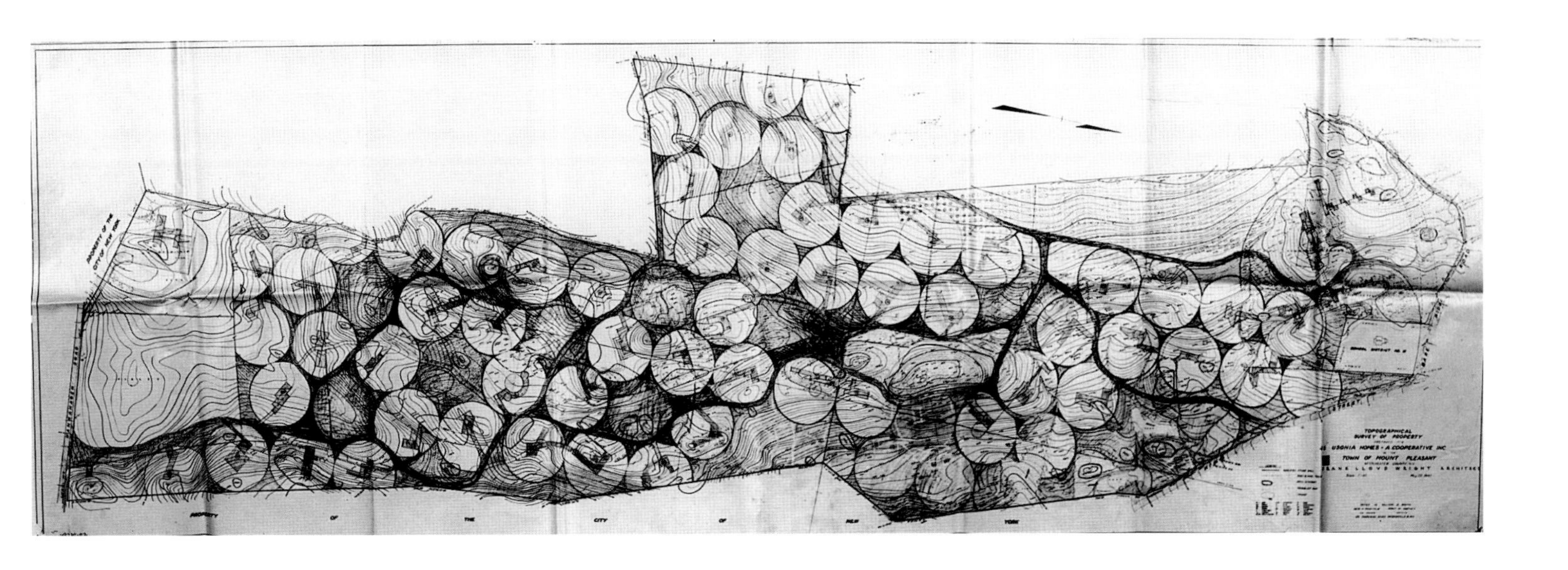

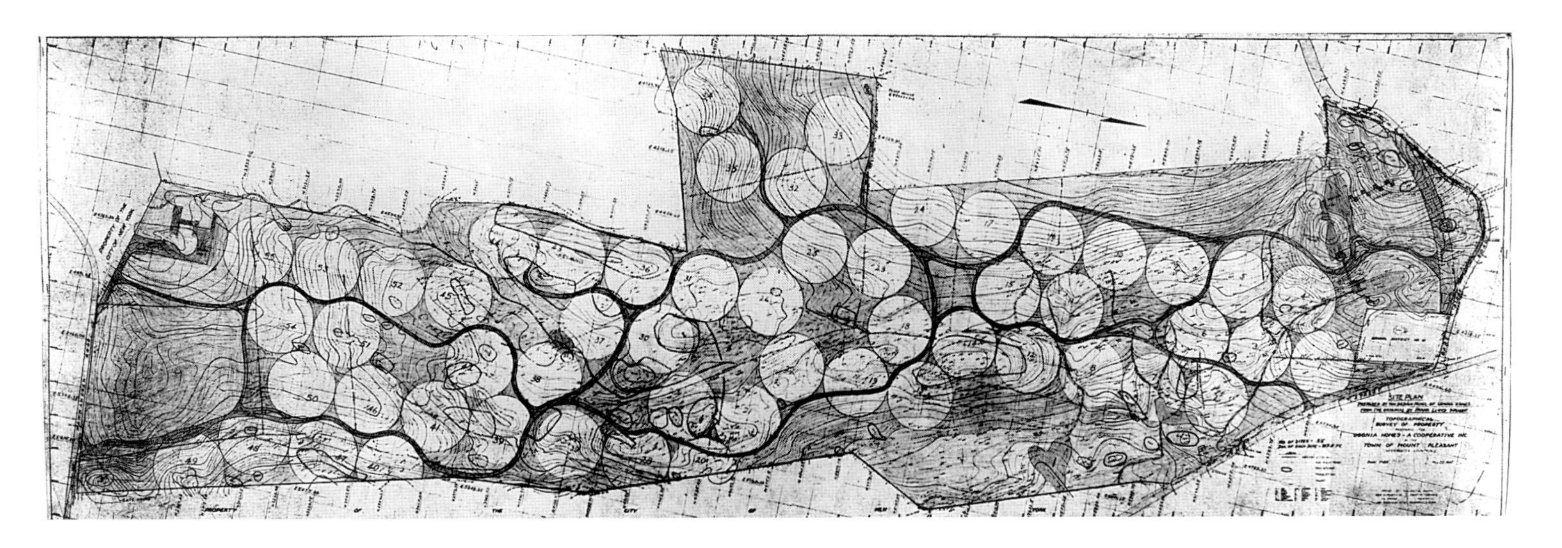

top: THE ORIGINAL SITE PLAN OF 1947 FEATURED CIRCULAR HOME SITES, NARROW WINDING ROADS, A FARM/RECREATION AREA AT THE SOUTH END, AND A COMMUNITY BUILDING AT THE NORTH END.

bottom: REVISED SITE PLAN: CIRCLES WERE ENLARGED FROM 200- TO 217-FOOT DIAMETER—A "BUILDER'S ACRE."

COURTESY THE FRANK LLOYD WRIGHT FOUNDATION, SCOTTSDALE, AZ

In the spring of 1947, with the land secured and design commencing, a more complete definition of the building committee's duties seemed necessary. On May 23, 1947, the membership approved a new plan to replace the building committee with an architectural association, which would be given comprehensive responsibility and authority for all aspects of design and architectural supervision, subject to approval by Wright. The association was soon called the "Design Panel" and was a partnership between Henken, Aaron Resnick (also an engineer and architect), and Kessler (though Kessler would soon withdraw).

Henken, as chief communicator with Wright, was absorbed with his association with Wright. He saw himself, correctly, as Wright's nearest and most authoritative representative. As founder of Usonia, he had a parent's protectiveness of both its concept and its reality. Henken was a man of tremendous energy, charisma, and ability, who was committed to act on his ideals. Out of a large group of fiercely idealistic people, he was perhaps the fiercest and most idealistic, and he worked himself into exhaustion for more than a decade to bring Usonia into reality.

The second pillar of the Design Panel was Aaron Resnick. Before joining Usonia, Resnick had worked as a structural engineer for the U.S. Navy. Though trained as an engineer, he was more interested in architecture. Believing that he was knowledgeable enough about architecture to attempt the New York State exams, he haggled with the authorities and eventually was allowed to take the tests. Despite never having taken an architectural course, he passed all seven parts of the rigorous examination at first go. Aaron and his wife Mildred were living with his parents in Brooklyn in 1944 when Mildred heard of Usonia. Aaron attended a meeting and became committed on the spot. By the end of 1945 he and Mildred had become members. Much like Frank Lloyd Wright, Resnick "deeply believed that architecture could help make this a better world, and that you had to live in cooperation to do it," Mildred said of her husband. "He felt that people could live in a symbiotic relationship with nature." Resnick would become a mainstay of the community and, like Henken, undertake a huge amount of labor for it.

In October 1947, a contract with the Design Panel—that is, Henken and Resnick—was presented to the membership for approval. It stipulated that they would "secure and provide the cooperative with all necessary architectural, engineering and design services in connection with the construction of a complete cooperative community." Other duties included serving as the liaison with Wright; hiring architects, engineers, and draftsmen as needed; holding conferences with owners; devising standards of design; preparing studies and detailed drawings for bids; keeping accounts; overseeing construction of not only the individual houses, but also of community buildings, park and playground areas, roads, and utilities; and providing all other services customarily rendered by an architect.

For their work the Design Panel would be paid two percent of the construction costs. Part of this fee was for on-site building supervision and for serving as intermediary between members and their architects. The other part was for their activities for the community rather than individual homes, such as selecting and procuring bulk materials and designing standard components like millwork, cabinets, and casement windows. Some members of the cooperative, however, strongly opposed approval of the

Design Panel contract. In a three-page letter, three board members, who soon resigned, stated:

> Our objections are based on what we feel to be serious deficiencies in the personnel of the Design Panel. We raise no question as to the architectural ingenuity and technical competence of the Design Panel members, and we do not doubt their personal honesty. We feel, however, that a lack of managerial ability and an extraordinary ineptness in the handling of group relations have been demonstrated during the precontractual existence of the Design Panel which makes us doubt the chances of survival of a business venture founded on such a basis.

Their reservations were not entirely without merit, perhaps not for the stated reasons, but for the magnitude of the delegated tasks. Henken and Resnick were being given contractual responsibility for the oversight, design, and construction of the *entire* community, despite their very limited experience. They would have to juggle not only the professional design issues, but also the personalities of many Usonians who fully expected to participate in the decision-making process. This was, after all, a co-op. Nevertheless, the Design Panel contract was approved at the membership meeting held on October 17, 1947, at the Blue Ribbon Restaurant, a convenient meeting place in Manhattan. Though a few people still had lingering reservations, most members thought that Wright's supervision would make up for Henken and Resnick's limited experience.

Even before they had a formal contract, Henken and Resnick had been at work informally working on details of the site plan and investigating the construction of roads, water system, sewage disposal, and electrical service. Well before the sites were established, several members asked to begin design of their homes. It was a very busy time for Henken and Resnick, and they had much to learn. They worked in Usonia's office—the living room of the New York apartment shared by the Henkens and the Podells—amid the clutter and confusion of Usonia's many other activities. "There were people that arrived at different times to work on their own or somebody else's project," recalled Henning Watterston, one of the many Taliesin apprentices who were welcome to stay at the apartment anytime. "The front door was hardly ever locked during the day and early evening. People came and went; the phone rang constantly." It had taken three years to reach this point. Somehow, a community emerged from this chaos.

HENKEN, AS CHIEF COMMUNICATOR WITH WRIGHT, WAS ABSORBED WITH HIS ASSOCIATION WITH WRIGHT. OUT OF A LARGE GROUP OF FIERCELY IDEALISTIC PEOPLE, HE WAS PERHAPS THE FIERCEST AND MOST IDEALISTIC.

One of the panel's most important tasks was to assemble a group of architects whose work would be acceptable to Wright. Wright declined to endorse any specific individuals, but did suggest a few names and, through a network of Taliesin acquaintances, others were identified. Formal agreements were made with, in addition to Henken and Resnick, Theodore Bower, Kaneji Domoto,

left: GROUNDBREAKING, 1948. MEMBERS WATCH START OF FOOTINGS FOR BEN HENKEN HOUSE. *© PEDRO E. GUERRERO*

above: MEMBERS UNLOAD AND STACK LUMBER FOR THE FIRST HOUSES. *© PEDRO E. GUERRERO*

Alden B. Dow, and Marcus Weston (all Taliesin Fellows) as well as Robert Bishop of Philadelphia, Paul Schweikher (Schweikher & Elting) of Roselle, Illinois, and Charles Warner (Warner and Leeds) of New Jersey. A second accepted group that informally expressed interest included Peter Berndtson, Cornelia Brierly, Gordon Chadwick, John Lautner, and Edgar Tafel (all Taliesin Fellows) as well as Bernard Kessler of Usonia and Delbert Larson. A few members wanted to use other architects than those on the list. The Design Panel opposed this but finally agreed that any architect could be employed provided Wright approved the design before the house could be built.

Resnick and Henken supported Usonia's goal to achieve a broad national sampling of architects, but they also wanted and needed design commissions themselves. Between them, Henken and Resnick designed twenty-six of Usonia's forty-seven homes. Not everyone was happy about this. Many thought there should be a wider representation of architects, and another list was suggested, but the advantages of having a local architect—also a member of Usonia—won out.

From the start Wright was gently skeptical of the Design Panel arrangements, although he went along with them. He believed that the panel was setting itself up for trouble by serving as the intermediary between the clients and the architects, as well as himself. Later, frustrated by the confusion that often ensued, Wright referred to it as the "Design Peril." In July 1947 he wrote to Henken suggesting a way to simplify the process:

> Make each architect accountable for the submission, acceptance, and execution of his project, subject only to the provisional veto in your contract with me. Urge standardizing of materials and millwork details so far as possible in order that mass buying may economize for all. Every sensible architect will be glad to do this. To insure good work with a free hand, remove all other lets and hindrances except the one I've mentioned.
>
> Too many "authorities" and "in-betweens" get things messy and become frustration [sic]. If the co-op is to become a building contractor that is all right. But the contractor should not control the architect at any point. To be sure the amateurs will need advice and restraint at many points but that should come from above them not below them.
>
> Send your boys to the vigilance committee. That's me.

The Design Panel was a source of strength and consistency in the early years of Usonia, and it helped ensure that the houses were truly organic. But the panel became a source of resentment and instability as well. There were conflicts among the Design Panel and members and architects. For Henken and Resnick not only reviewed plans for houses, passing or rejecting designs as they saw fit; they also administered and organized work for which the cooperative as well as individual members paid them.

This arrangement aimed for fairness, since the work was difficult and called for paid professional expertise. An expert panel was a practical necessity: it would have been impossible for the assembled cooperative to vote on each technical issue of design and construction. Nor would it have been fair to expect free work from experts. Both Henken and Resnick forwent more lucrative work for the sake of Usonia. But ambiguity remained. Financial issues also added problems. Cost overruns are a feature of any building project, and, unbeknown to them, Usonians were about to build in a decade during which housing and building costs would quadruple. Disagreements over costs and fees resulted in anger and estrangement among several Usonians.

The community was in a constant state of flux as some members moved to other cities or changed jobs or had more children. Only eleven of the thirty families who had originally committed to Usonia remained to build. Departing members were not quickly replaced, and returning their investment was almost impossible, since much of the money had already been spent.

By late fall of 1947, although there was still no financing, Usonians were determined to start preparing the land for roads, water, and electricity. Most members wanted to start design of their homes as quickly as possible. The transition from planning to construction was imminent and a source of anxiety as well as enthusiasm.

But reservations about this, as well as other issues, characterized Usonia's progression toward realization. An element of abstraction in the shared concepts allowed varying visions of the reality—the actual location of the land. the actual cost to build, and so on. When it was time to commit to the Design Panel and begin construction, not all members agreed on how to proceed. In December six concerned members distributed a lengthy communication of philosophy, analysis, and criticism. They felt the board was not working harmoniously and was not informing the membership of critical matters. They complained that the board was meeting only one night a week and urged the board to resign for a reorganization. Two directors did resign from the board and Usonia. They were replaced by Ralph Miller and deBlois Bush, who joined President Jack Masson, Vice President Odif Podell, and Treasurer Ben Henken. This was a committed board, determined to move ahead together.

HOW THE ECONOMY NEARLY DESTROYED USONIA

The unpredictable inflationary economy of the era wreaked havoc with the costs and estimates of the Usonians. After the war building boomed in the United States as never before, driving up the cost of materials and construction. A house that was reasonably priced for a middle-class American family in 1943 was all but out of reach a few years later. This spelled real trouble for Usonians, as Priscilla Henken later acknowledged: "Basing our ideas on prewar costs, we aimed too high without realizing that houses would quadruple in cost."

Usonia was still unable to get mortgage financing. Banks would not give mortgages on homes that were owned by a cooperative. And the clause in Usonia's by-laws calling for a nondenominational, multiethnic, multiracial community—hardly a characteristic of suburban neighborhood in the 1940s—frightened would-be mortgagers; a community that included Jews, atheists, socialists, and blacks might bring down property values. Despite concerted efforts, after Arthur Boyer withdrew in 1949, Usonia was never able to enroll African-American families. (Usonia's first black member-owner joined in 1999.) And banks were suspicious of the new construction techniques and modern designs of the houses; they feared that the homes would sell poorly. Some banks made these biases fairly explicit in their correspondence, and others couched them in business terms. Prejudice was not the only, or perhaps even the main, force at work. Usonia was simply too new and untried. "It all seemed so simple until we actually attempted to get money," Priscilla Henken recalled.

One institution had suggested it was willing to give mortgages, but only for finished houses. And so after tumultuous meetings of late 1947 and early 1948, Usonia came to a momentous decision to pool the money it had on hand—about $120,000, most of it from members' accounts, some of it borrowed—to help finance the building of five houses to show that it could be done, that Usonia was real. Herb Brandon was an especially influential voice in this decision. "I felt that until we got some houses up, we would never get building loans and mortgages," he later explained.

The cooperative and five families agreed upon the estimated prices for their homes as a group. Labor and material costs were to be recorded for each home. It was also understood that construction of these houses would share some costs equally between them and provide training for the architects, builders, and workmen, some part of which would be paid for by Usonia, presumably to make future construction more efficient and less costly. This scheme, which led to such difficulties later, effectively took the costs out of the families' hands—thus rendering them vulnerable in ways that none of them anticipated. After some debate, the board decided to "build two in the north, three in the south." They were the Resnick and Benzer homes, designed by Aaron Resnick, and the Ben Henken (David's father), Kepler, and Miller homes, designed by David Henken.

1948 GROUNDBREAKING, AT LAST

The Design Panel completed working drawings for the roads according to Wright's site plan and soon let a contract to construct the first three thousand feet. These private internal roads were narrow, only sixteen feet wide in a few places. The community's construction headquarters was a $500 war surplus Quonset hut, obtained from the Eastern Cooperative League. Usonia's embrace of cooperative principles had evolved from total commitment to general acceptance with focus on anticipated benefits to a housing association. Usonia did obtain some lumber and one hundred kegs of nails, but little else was available that met Usonia's needs. To keep costs down Usonia purchased some materials in quantity: a carload of structural lumber, a carload of Rayduct (pipe for the radiant heat systems) from Bethlehem Steel, forty thousand bricks, a carload of cast iron drain pipe, and a carload of one-inch cypress.

The Design Panel held discussions with General Electric about obtaining boilers at a discount, and set up meetings with heating and plumbing contractors. Westchester Lighting (the local electric company) demanded substantial payment to bring power into Usonia until, in the spring of 1949, the Public Service Commission ruled that they were obliged to provide service. Wright and the Usonians wanted underground wiring, and noted Wright's comments on the subject: "There is no such thing as a charming place or a beautiful place with poles and wires.... What is the use of building these beautiful homes if we create the same old slum?... Underground lines are the first condition of a modern improvement." But the power company adamantly refused despite repeated efforts. (Later, members installed underground wiring from poles on their own property to their houses.) The technical committee had seriously explored the possibility of Usonia generating its own electricity, but concluded it was not practical.

By early spring Henken and Resnick had completed drawings for several houses and sent them to builders for bids. Board member Sol Friedman wrote a letter to co-op members in April 1948 informing them of the progress:

FRANK LLOYD WRIGHT "DISCUSSING" SAND, IN FRONT OF THE DAVID HENKEN HOUSE (UNDER CONSTRUCTION), 1949. THE PHOTO INCLUDES DESIGN PANEL MEMBERS AARON RESNICK (WITH GLASSES) AND DAVID HENKEN (WITH BEARD) STANDING NEXT TO WRIGHT, AS WELL AS (FROM LEFT TO RIGHT) BERT AND SOL FRIEDMAN, BOBBIE AND SID MILLER, ED SERLIN (BEHIND BOBBIE), AN UNIDENTIFIED WOMAN, AND BUILDER ROBERT CHUCKROW (FACING AWAY). *© PEDRO E. GUERRERO*

HOUSES BUILT WITH POOLED CO-OP FUNDS TO DEMONSTRATE THE PRACTICALITY OF USONIAN HOUSES.

clockwise from top left: BEN HENKEN HOUSE UNDER CONSTRUCTION, 1949, BY DAVID HENKEN FOR HIS PARENTS. *© PEDRO E. GUERRERO;* JOHN KEPLER HOUSE BY DAVID HENKEN, UNDER CONSTRUCTION, 1949; RALPH MILLER HOUSE BY DAVID HENKEN, UNDER CONSTRUCTION, 1949; AARON RESNICK HOUSE NEARING COMPLETION, SPRING 1949.

LATTER THREE PHOTOS BY HENRY RAPISARDA, COSMO-SILEO ASSOCIATES

RADIANT HEATING, USED IN NEARLY ALL OF WRIGHT'S BUILDINGS AFTER 1936, WAS A HALLMARK OF USONIA'S HOMES. THE BETHLEHEM STEEL COMPANY PHOTOGRAPHED BENDING AND WELDING PIPE FROM USONIA'S CARLOAD OF RAYDUCT. ***from far left:*** BENDING THE RAYDUCT; WELDING THE JOINTS; DAVID HENKEN PREPARING FOR GRAVEL BASE. *ALL PHOTOS COURTESY BETHLEHEM STEEL COMPANY*

> Dear Usonian;
>
> Working drawings of the first few houses are in the hands of builders at this time.... Costs are higher than was anticipated.... Many of us will not be able to build if the rise is excessive.... The first group of houses will provide the data on which the houses to be built later will be planned. Everything that can be done to reduce the out-of-pocket costs on this group... will mean "more house" for those of us who build later.... We have informed the builders that they are not to include any figure for site clearing in their estimate.... We know that the clearing can be done by our own Co-operative group....
>
> Organized work on the sites for the first houses will start on Saturday, April 17th, and will continue every Saturday and Sunday thereafter.
>
> Co-operatively yours,
> Land Improvements Committee
> Sol Friedman

The shared "let's build it" commitment energized and bonded the Usonians in 1948 and 1949 as they coped with the challenge of their new venture. Together they would monitor construction as well as do some of the work, but they needed professional builders. They sought advice from one of the most experienced supervisors of Wright's Usonian houses—Harold Turner. Turner had been "discovered" by Paul and Jean Hanna, Wright clients who built a home in Palo Alto, California, in the late 1930s. After receiving some training and the approval of Frank Lloyd Wright, Turner actively supervised the construction of the Hanna's Usonian home based on a hexagonal module, a unique design that was widely hailed for its contribution to American architecture. Turner went on to supervise the building of other Wright houses and was regarded by many as "Mr. Wright's builder."

In April 1948, Usonia invited Turner to visit for two weeks to consult on its building program plans. Several prospective builders including Turner were interviewed and Robert Chuckrow Construction Company of Hartsdale, New York, was selected. Chuckrow—an educated, cultivated man—had a real appreciation for Wrightian architecture, and therefore more than purely commercial interest in building this project and building it well. His father had helped to build the Chrysler Building in New York. Although his company was small, Chuckrow agreed to bring in specialty services and manpower as needed. But he, along with almost everyone else associated with the project, underestimated its difficulty. The many strong personalities involved were one complication—but Chuckrow would also encounter innovative plans, new materials, and unfamiliar specifications. He was faced with an extremely diverse group of houses and architects, some relatively new to the business of building real houses.

Meanwhile, most of the committed members had already selected architects and design was proceeding. In addition to Henken and Resnick, the designers of the first fourteen homes included Schweikher and Elting, Kaneji Domoto, and Frank Lloyd Wright. In May drawings for three more houses were completed.

Four families—Ottilie and Irwin Auerbach, Florence and Arthur Boyer, Bert and Sol Friedman, and Bobbie and Sid Miller—had already requested that Wright design houses for them. "We are aware," Henken wrote to Wright, "you have limited yourself to five"—which had been Wright's original stipulation—"and reserve the right to reject any of them for your own reasons." Later, Wright would offer to design more. When financial problems began to crop up, Wright was interested in making available some of his "Usonian Automatics"—prefabricated houses of standardized design and materials, meant to be owner built.

On July 10, 1948, Henken wrote to Wright that "10,000 feet of road has been bulldozed, two thirds of which is graded and covered with crushed rock.... Several houses have been staked and bulldozed, and a few have put forth their first tender shoots of footings, trenches, piers, and walls.... Usonia is out of its infancy and taking its first toddling steps."

THIS CRITICAL PERIOD IS IRONICALLY THE ONE THAT SURVIVING USONIANS REMEMBER WITH GREATEST FONDNESS. THE COOPERATIVE WAS VERY NEAR TO COLLAPSE. IT HAD WAGERED ALL ITS COLLECTIVE RESOURCES ON BUILDING ITS FIRST FIVE HOUSES.

USONIA AS AN EXTENDED FAMILY

This critical period is ironically the one that surviving Usonians remember with greatest fondness. The cooperative was very near to collapse. It had wagered all its collective resources on building its first five houses, and it was in arrears to many suppliers and subcontractors. Yet many Usonians were commuting into the woods, rain or shine, to help with construction. They knew they had to combine forces to ensure the success of the project and keep costs down. On weekends city dwellers would faithfully show up in overalls with tools in hand, ready for heavy labor. A November 1948 newsletter article by Jack Wax captured one memorable workday:

> Lunch on the Podell Terrace... did you have your lunch there last Sunday? You should have. After putting in a full morning's work, foreman Johnny Kepler blew his whistle and about 15 families gathered on the terrace for a picnic. This was cooperation at its best and it would have done your heart good to see everyone working together for the common good.... The work is again lined up for this weekend. Everyone will be assigned a task; the biggest one now is cleaning up the sites.... This is our chance to get a head start—and lessen the cost of your house and mine.

Not only did this cooperation speed the building of the houses, it also cemented Usonia as a community. The wheelbarrow, that important symbol, was joined by the picnic basket. Usonians turned cooperative construction into social occasions, with children scrambling around construction sites, and friends and neighbors, Usonian or not, hauled along to help. In turn, social get-togethers often turned into technical consultations as neighbors helped move materials, wire rooms, and cover roofs. "You couldn't really call them parties usually," Usonian Trude Victor said. "We'd all sooner or later end up in the boiler room or on the roof."

Rowland and Fay Watts recalled the pride of helping to build their own house: Fay "held up one end of

FOURTEEN PAGES SUNDAY, OCTOBER 10, 1948

Co-operative Project Rising Under Supervision of Frank Lloyd Wright

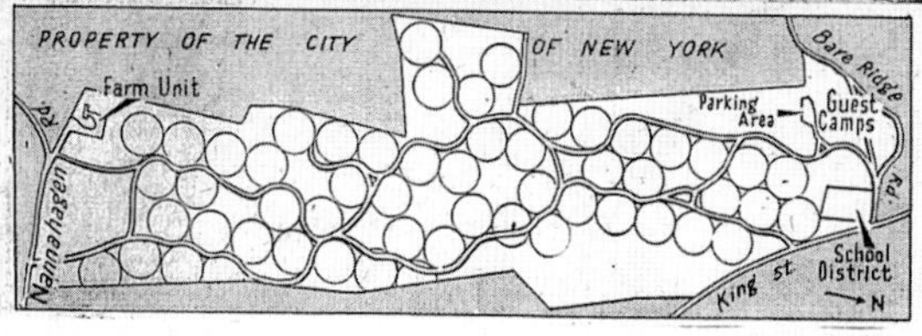

Cosmo-Sileo Associates

Shown above is a two-bedroom house designed by David Henkin for Usonia Homes, a community of more than fifty dwellings near Pleasantville, N. Y. At left is a diagram of the unique circular home sites

Westchester Colony Uses Circular Lots

Frank Lloyd Wright Plans Co-operative Project Near Pleasantville

By Frederick Gutheim

SAMUEL BUTLER first called us Usonians, saying that citizens of the United States took in too much territory when they called themselves Americans. But it remained for Frank Floyd Wright, the Wisconsin architect, to give the term usage. In the form of Usonia Homes, a housing co-operative of fifty dwellings now being built under Mr. Wright's supervision near Pleasantville in Westchester County, Mr. Butler's term is being affixed to the land for the first time.

No one would expect from Mr. Wright anything in the ordinary as housing developments go. An iconoclast whose prejudices have been fully ventilated, as in opposition to Radio City or as the creator of the challenging Guggenheim Museum, the architect's heterodoxy, extends to every phase of building. Here it begins with the land.

Instead of a conventional subdivision, Mr. Wright has elected to use a series of circular tracts, each one acre in size. On paper they satisfy, and who sees property lines except on paper in this sort of development? The tedious legal descriptions of property by metes and bounds are reduced to one point and a radius. One further advantage is that the property of any two owners touches only in the realm of mathematical theory; in fact it always abuts on common land of the housing co-operative. About half of the co-operatively owned tract of ninety-seven acres of wooded land at the north end of the Kensico Reservoir is held in common, fifty-five acres being devoted to home sites.

Private Ownership Curbed

The circular lots device has been used before by the architect in another co-operative housing project at Okemos, Mich., and for this type of development it has much to recommend it. It is the antithesis of conventional land ownership, which Mr. Wright abhors. It reduces private ownership to a perfunctory formality, and should provide a litmus paper test of the co-operators' intentions.

Also to be held in common by the group are two open plots at either end of the development. Consistent with his ideas of residential seclusion, the designer has chosen to use these as buffers, instead of locating them at the

(Continued on page 2, column 6)

What Are Usonia Homes Like?

Under the supervision of well known architect Frank Lloyd Wright a housing co-operative of fifty dwellings —"Usonia Homes"—is now being built near Pleasantville in Westchester County. The project offers substantial privacy and independence, plus a large measure of co-operative services. Houses will be occupied mostly by young, middle-income professional people. For Frederick Gutheim's description of something new in housing developments . . . see Section V, the Real Estate and Home Section . . . of

Tomorrow's New York Herald Tribune

ARTICLE APPEARING IN THE *NEW YORK HERALD TRIBUNE*, OCTOBER 10, 1948. NEWS OF USONIA WAS FEATURED IN NEWSPAPERS ALL OVER THE UNITED STATES. *COLLECTION ROLAND REISLEY*

a board for the living room ceiling while Rowland nailed in the other end. While that was over forty years ago, the ceiling is still intact." Betsy Glass said, "I remember the Quonset hut, cement mixers, and nails; the smells of fresh lumber, tar paper, wet concrete." And Julia Brody recalled "weekends during which [her husband] George, as part of a brigade, trundled wheelbarrow loads of gravel needed to create beds for the radiant heat coils for the first group of houses. There were times when I thought the wheelbarrow was an appendage to his arms."

Members did not expect to be paid for their weekend work at the land. Some however planned to do substantial work on their own homes and, since their equity in Usonia was the amount of their investment, they felt that they should be credited with the fair market value of their work. This was accepted in principle, but in detail it entailed much discussion and many pages of evaluation and analysis. A "Committee to Analyze Credit for Member Work" was established and a motion passed that any objection to their findings be reported to the membership. Although such work was done by some members, few, if any, made requests for credit. Perhaps the requests were deferred and in due course became academic. The paid workmen at Usonia were union members and there was concern that they might object to work being done by Usonians; however that did not occur.

The Usonians, all city folk, were unused to and in some cases fearful of the challenges of country life. The land committee initiated a poison ivy control plan and the head keeper of reptiles at the Central Park Zoo spent a whole day at the land looking for reported snakes. He said there were "positively no dangerous reptiles in the vicinity." In fact there was the occasional rattlesnake and copperhead, but no one was bitten and after a few years they disappeared.

The Design Panel completed specifications for the water system and estimated it would cost $40,000. Chuckrow, however, said he could do it for less, providing that members prepare trenches and lay pipe. Members did manage to help a bit. As activity increased Chuckrow hired a building superintendent, Charles Weinberg, and Usonia hired a clerk of the works, Murray Smith, to expedite building, check progress, and oversee bills. In retrospect, control of the construction process was often inefficient, even chaotic. Thinking that they could reduce costs, Usonians themselves wanted to approve purchases and verify deliveries and work completed. Usonian George Brody, who was also a CPA, worked with the board, the Design Panel, and Chuckrow in repeated attempts to accomplish this.

Members were often at the sites with comments or criticism and were admonished to bring them to the building committee or Design Panel, not the workmen. The Design Panel said it must be able to authorize changes in the field, but Chuckrow, concerned with their impact on costs, had been permitted to delay the implementation of changes pending review. He was to advise the board if he disagreed with a change and the Design Panel was to keep records of changes and their cost. Construction was further complicated at times when there was no money to pay a supplier or meet the payroll. Several times members were informed that the carpenters or masons or Design Panel draftsmen were laid off and reminded that arrears in their own accounts amounted to $30,000. When there was not enough cash to continue building homes, the little bit left was placed in a utility fund to continue work on the water system.

PUMP HOUSE. IN JANUARY 1949 MEMBERS COLLECTED STONES FROM THE LAND FOR THIS FIRST STRUCTURE BUILT IN USONIA. MEMBERS ALSO HELPED TO LAY PIPE IN TRENCHES FOR THE WATER SYSTEM. ELECTRICITY AND WATER WERE AVAILABLE AT THE END OF JUNE, JUST DAYS BEFORE THE FIRST RESIDENTS MOVED IN.

THE BUILDERS OF INSANIA

Nevertheless the houses were being built. Chuckrow said he was paying less than expected for material but labor was higher than estimated due to the high standards required and workers' unfamiliarity with the building system. Indeed, local carpenters who worked on Usonia's houses came to refer to the community as "Insania." To some workers the guiding principles of the cooperative seemed crazy and the architecture alien. For the first time in some careers their workmanship was being challenged. Sometimes this resulted in work of the first order as they rose to the task. In other cases it led to slowdowns, confusion, and added cost.

Workmen were often faced with unfamiliar "Wrightian" elements such as mitered plate glass windows that terminated in masonry walls and many angular joints of sixty or one-hundred-twenty degrees rather than conventional right angles. Many structural components that were usually covered or painted were the final exterior or interior surface; these exposed areas called for unusual precision.

Much of the work required extraordinary attention to detail, which seemed at conflict with the original idea to save costs through standardization and simplification. Nevertheless, a cadre of the construction crew, including head carpenter Jack Dennerlein and chief mason Nick Sardelli, became proud of their participation in work they felt was significant and beautiful. Years later they would bring friends and family to the site and recall Wright's instruction and comments.

Wright was never too enthusiastic about the work of any builders but his own. When he visited Usonia he showed irritation when things were not exactly right, and mild surprise when things were done well. Head carpenter Dennerlein recalled that Wright "expected workmen to know exactly what was demanded of them, even with his unusual designs. He would be intolerant of a carpenter, for instance, who might ask how something was to be done." Dennerlein, however, found Wright "likeable" and "marvelously clever."

Harold Turner was asked back in September 1948 to help handle some of the problems. He said the workmen were good but needed more supervision and that the Design Panel should supply field drawings to avoid misunderstanding. Turner was to return again in early October to demonstrate the laying of a concrete floor slab. Frank Lloyd Wright, expected at the same time, suggested a picnic with members.

Work on the water system continued. Members carried pipe and placed it in the trenches. A pump house was needed at the well, so they gathered field stones and brought them to the site where masons soon constructed a small building, the first to be completed in Usonia. The water gushed at forty-five gallons per minute from the Artesian well, which, with a suitable storage tank, was judged sufficient for the community. Although the well was central and near a high point of the community, a water tower was needed for adequate pressure. Its height would slightly exceed the zoning limits, and hence require a variance. Once again Judge Kenyon would call on her friend Ed Cox, who obtained the consent of Senator Mastick, Usonia's neighbor to the west.

The members agreed to community financing for two additional homes and, responding to seven members who were willing to pursue independent financing, the board authorized bulldozing and footings for nine more houses. With houses nearing completion and others started, Usonia had become tangible and hundreds of curious visitors from near and far came to see the novel community. Though they were welcomed as a potential source of new members, as well as pride, they effected additional access controls. Soon signs and gates were erected and informational brochures were written to hand out to prospective new Usonians.

In June 1949 the negotiation of easements and a contract with Westchester Lighting concluded. The company's poles were installed and wiring proceeded. Electricity would be available to most homes by mid-July. With the water tower completed and water service connected, it was time for the first Usonians to move in. At the July 11 meeting of the board of directors, Rowland Watts made the following motion, "Having received a satisfactory letter of application from Aaron and Mildred Resnick, the board authorizes them to move into the house erected on site fifty-two, on July 13." Usonia was becoming a reality at last.

Chapter Four A COMMUNITY AT LAST

ON JULY 13, 1949, AARON AND MILDRED RESNICK MOVED INTO A HOUSE IN THE WOODS WITHOUT CLOSETS, DOORS, OR FINISHED CEILINGS. THEIR FAMILY SLEPT IN THE LIVING ROOM. THEY WERE SOON FOLLOWED BY JOHN AND JEAN KEPLER ON JULY 20, SYDNEY AND FLORENCE BENZER ON THE 22ND, RALPH AND CLARA MILLER ON THE 29TH, AND ROWLAND AND FAY WATTS ON AUGUST 9. THESE FAMILIES, ALONG WITH SEVEN OTHERS BY THE END OF THE YEAR AND MANY THAT CAME LATER, MOVED INTO HOMES THAT TO ONE DEGREE OR another were unfinished. "We lived with a pile of lumber in the living room for some while. It didn't hold us back," recalled Fay Watts. "We even had parties with guests sitting on the piles of cypress instead of chairs." Many members did some of their own work, such as filling nail holes and applying wax or varnish. Some even became experts on the job.

That winter a huge snowstorm cut off road access and electricity for days and effectively isolated the first families. They began to worry about finding milk for their children, and so struck an agreement with the nearby Orbaek Dairy. Orbaek's horse-drawn sleigh carried the milk to Palmer Lane, about three-fourths of a mile from the community, and Usonian John Kepler would load the milk into a sled, haul it to Usonia, and distribute it. Usonians were learning to adjust to life in the country.

Once the first houses were up, socializing continued among Usonia's extended family. The annealing trial by fire of construction under pressure, the intensity of the financial risks, and the relief of sharing the anxiety as well as the commitment with like-minded neighbors-to-be forged an unusual closeness. This was the stage at which Usonia became a community. "Once we were settled in our homes, there was a good deal of visiting among us and as I now think of it an obvious sense of trust," Usonian Julia Brody explained. "Extended family was indeed family and trust did abound among us."

When some Usonians were having financial problems, they found ways to see them through, sometimes by mysterious means. "At one point in the early days I didn't have enough to feed my family much less keep building the house," recalled Jack Masson. "I was about to

A LIGHT MOMENT ON THE BALCONY OF THE BENZER HOUSE, 1949. RESNICK, WRIGHT, SERLIN, AND FRIEDMAN.

HENRY RAPISARDA, COSMO-SILEO ASSOCIATES

resign when a check for $1000 came with a note saying I could pay it back without interest when I wanted to." Masson, who had secured permission to build his own house, designed by David Henken, was not the only Usonian to benefit from such anonymous largesse. Through the years the cooperative maintained a semiofficial slush fund for members' use. As late as 1971 a newspaper reporter could write that "a fund still exists, but nobody knows who borrows how much from it. Help is offered when it seems needed without being asked for." Only Usonian Herb Brandon knew. He was the "invisible" collector/dispenser of such assistance. Some members also borrowed from each other.

The euphoria of creating the beautiful homes and the growing bonds among the Usonians, however, was tempered by serious continuing problems. Usonia Homes still had no mortgage financing; costs were exceeding every estimate; and some members felt forced to withdraw and demanded return of their investment—which had been spent. Despite much interest and curiosity from the outside, recruiting and retaining urgently needed new members was difficult.

THE PIONEERS

That Usonia survived its birth pains was undoubtedly due to its most active pioneers. At the outset these included David Henken and his wife Priscilla, a teacher; David's sister Judeth, a Social Service secretary, and her husband Odif Podell, an industrial engineer; Priscilla's sister Julia, a librarian, and her husband George Brody, a CPA. Other key members by 1946 were Aaron Resnick, a structural engineer and Henken's partner in the Design Panel; Murry Gabel, a teacher and insurance broker; and Jack Masson, an insurance salesman and co-op/union activist. In 1947 Sidney Benzer, a dentist, Ralph Miller, a chemical engineer, Herbert Brandon, a trade paper publisher, John Kepler, a craftsman, and Rowland Watts, a civil rights and labor lawyer, all joined and played significant roles. Others who were active contributors but were unable to remain with the community included Bernard Kessler, an engineer and architect, John Troll, an engineer, Bernard Attinson, a co-op activist and optometrist, deBlois Bush, the *Newsonian* editor, secretary, and business manager, and Sidney Hertzberg, a journalist.

From the very beginning in 1944 to the start of construction in 1948, this group, along with their wives, was the foundation of the community that followed. The women at the time did not serve as directors or on the legal, technical, and financial committees, though they chaired the very significant membership and social committees, and were active participants at board, membership, and other meetings.

New members who joined in 1948 and remained to build homes included Sol Friedman, a book and music store owner, and his wife Bert; Arthur Bier, a physician and amateur violinist, and his wife Gertrude; Max Victor, a leather importer and artist, and his wife Trude; Jesse Lurie, a journalist, and his wife Irene; Bill Harris, an engineer, and his wife Esther; Sidney Miller, a textile executive, and his wife Barbara; Jack Wax, a magazine editor, and his wife, Anne; Al Scheinbaum, a book dealer, and his wife Lucille; John Silson, a physician, and his wife Dorothy; Jacob Hillesum, a diamond expert, and his wife Lisette; Edward Glass, a furniture executive, and his wife Istar; James Anderson, a chemist, and his wife Marjorie; Edward Serlin, a publicist, and his wife Beatrice; Isaiah Lew, a den-

AARON RESNICK HOUSE

clockwise from bottom left: FLOOR PLAN *REDRAWN BY TOBIAS GUGGENHEIMER STUDIO*; VIEW OF SOUTH FACADE; THE INTERIOR EXHIBITS USONIAN "VOCABULARY": OPEN WORKSPACE, CLERESTORY WINDOWS, NATURAL BRICK, CYPRESS, AND MODULAR, RED CONCRETE FLOOR *© ROLAND REISLEY, ASSISTED BY HOWARD MILLER*

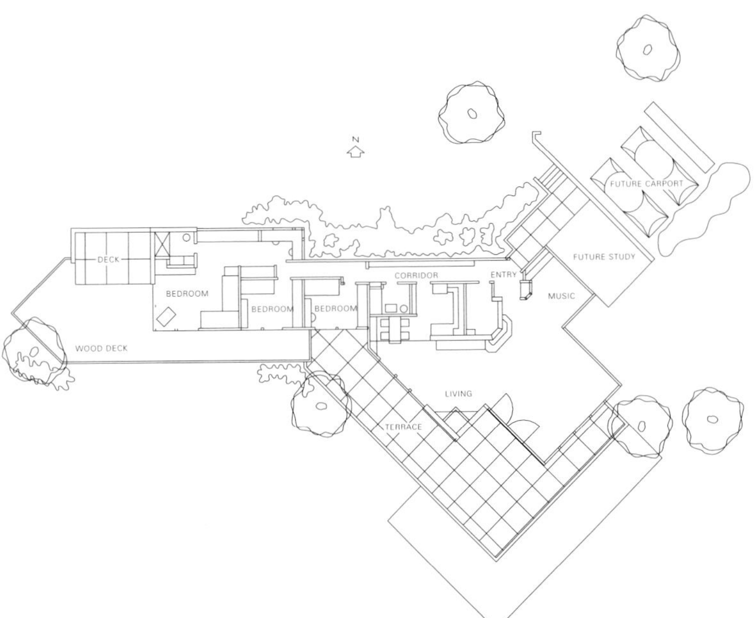

FEATURE STORIES, ILLUSTRATED WITH THE FRANK LLOYD WRIGHT SITE PLAN AND PHOTOS OF EARLY HOUSES, APPEARED IN *ARCHITECTURAL FORUM, HOUSE AND GARDEN,* THE *NEW YORK TIMES,* AND THE *HERALD TRIBUNE.*

tist, and his wife Charlotte; and Irwin Auerbach, an auditor, and his wife Ottalie.

Efforts to attract new members continued and several joined, but between 1948 and 1951, Roland Reisley, the author of this book and then a physicist, and his wife Ronny, a psychologist, were the only permanent new members.

SEEKING NEW MEMBERS

While the board focused on building and seeking finance during 1948 and 1949, other members selected and worked with their architects, and everyone was concerned with the need to enroll additional members. Visitors to the land were almost always invited to explore membership. Press releases added to the considerable media attention.

Publicity for Usonia was greatly enhanced when, in January 1948, Edward Serlin became a member. Serlin was the director of publicity for Radio City Music Hall and promptly assumed that task for Usonia as well. Soon stories about Usonia began appearing in newspapers and magazines all over the country. Feature stories, illustrated with the Frank Lloyd Wright site plan and photos of early houses, appeared in *Architectural Forum, House and Garden,* the *New York Times,* and the *Herald Tribune* as well as other local and national papers. The returns from a clipping service soon filled a scrapbook.

Hardly the most prominent, but the most remembered story was an article in the newspaper *PM* on April 25, 1948. *PM* was a liberal-leaning New York afternoon paper aimed at a more serious reader than the popular tabloids. The article resulted in five hundred inquiries and a number of meetings with applicants, several of whom became members of Usonia.

THE CHUCKROW REPORT

Even as new members were recruited and new houses were planned, cost overruns became a serious issue. Late in 1949, Usonia's builder, Robert Chuckrow, submitted a comprehensive report regarding building progress to that point and suggested future improvements. Chuckrow had hoped to build the first ten to fifteen houses as a group to achieve some economy of scale. But he found this was not to be. He had to deal with the Design Panel, the architects, the intensely concerned owners, and activist board and committee members. All had forged enthusiastically into unknown territory.

Chuckrow noted that during this period "many troubles" had been endured and overcome. The cost of materials, especially masonry materials, steel and rough hardware, plumbing, and heating supplies had increased since inception, while the cost of lumber had decreased.

Chuckrow called supervision a "confusing" matter probably not "understood by all parties." He especially pleaded with architects to spend more time "preparing complete and accurate drawings." All of the first five houses

THE *NEW YORK TIMES* DESCRIBED UNUSUAL FEATURES, INCLUDING RADIANT HEATING, OF USONIAN HOMES NEARING COMPLETION. *NEW YORK TIMES*

TUESDAY, MAY 17, 1949. The New York Times

A NEW COOPERATIVE HOUSING DEVELOPMENT UNDER WAY IN WESTCHESTER COUNTY

Checking the window encasements on one of the homes being erected in Mount Pleasant Township.

Mr. and Mrs. John Kepler and their children on the porch of their prospective residence.

NEW KIND OF HOME RISING IN SUBURBS

Solar Houses on Round Lots, Minus Attics, Cellars, Mark Big Westchester Project

By MERRILL FOLSOM

Special to THE NEW YORK TIMES.

PLEASANTVILLE, N. Y., May 16—A residential neighborhood of tomorrow that sets a new pace in modern architecture and cooperative ownership is rising from ninety-seven acres of wooded hillside and rolling meadow in Central Westchester.

The colony has been designed by Frank Lloyd Wright of Wisconsin and Arizona, silver-haired exponent of "organic modernism," and it is already becoming a mecca for planning students of many nations.

Its features include round lots, solar houses, radiant heating, free-flowing interiors, wall-size fireplaces, cantilever roofs, extra-broad terraces, spacious gardens and large expanses of glass that can be opened to integrate the indoors with the world outside.

Going over the radiant heated floors of one of the homes which is piped for hot water to provide warmth. Left to right: Dr. Sidney Benzer, owner; Jack Dennerlin, construction foreman, and Aaron Resnick, designer. Looking on is Mrs. Benzer.

The New York Times (by Edward Hausner)

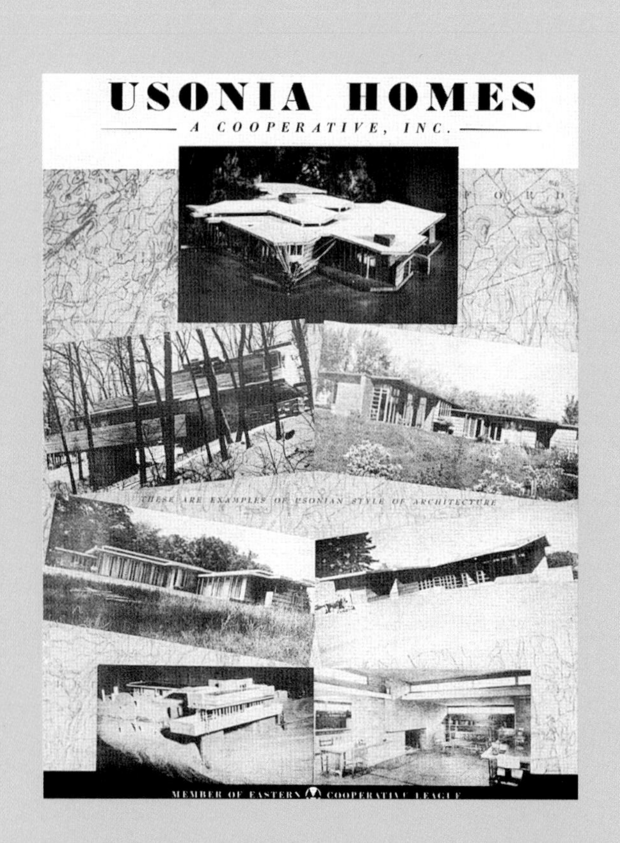

left: IN 1947 THE REVISED USONIA BROCHURE AGAIN PICTURED WRIGHT DESIGNS. NOTE EASTERN COOP LEAGUE MEMBERSHIP. *COLLECTION ROLAND REISLEY*

right: WATTS HOUSE, 1949, BY SCHWEIKHER & ELTING WAS AMONG THE FIRST FIVE OCCUPIED. USONIA'S LAST BROCHURE IN 1950 FEATURED THIS PHOTOGRAPH. *WALTER A. SLATTERY*

BEN HENKEN HOUSE, 1949

left: THIS PHOTO WAS WIDELY SEEN IN THE PUBLICITY ON THE COMMUNITY AFTER MORTGAGE FINANCING BY THE KNICKERBOCKER BANK. *WALTER A. SLATTERY*

right: FLOOR PLAN. *REDRAWN BY TOBIAS GUGGENHEIMER STUDIO*

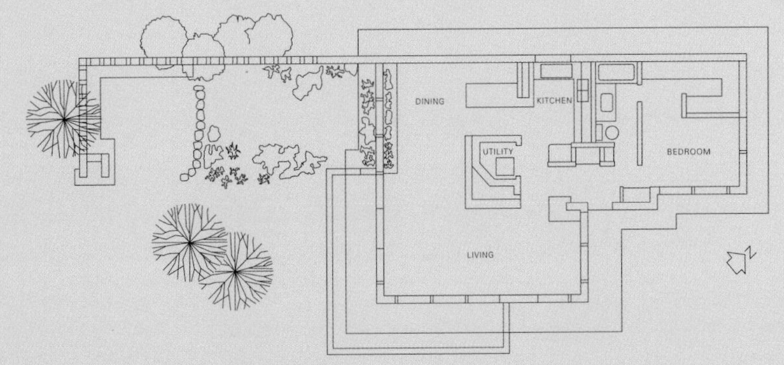

were drawn to incomplete plans, making the builder's duties more complicated than normal. Original specifications "were so modified... that they became useless."

Chuckrow's remarks reveal the way Usonia at first tried to operate: that is, with frequent, detailed meetings and massive changes of mind on all sides all the time. "Once the owner accepts the completed drawings," Chuckrow wrote, he or she should not "demand subsequent revisions by the architect." And, completed drawings are "proof" that the architect is "satisfied" with the plans and that nothing will be changed except in an emergency. Clearly, both owners and architects had been making changes right up to and past the time building began.

Above all, Chuckrow asked members of Usonia "to face the situation honestly." No "magic system" of building is inherent in Usonian architecture, he explained. Its emphasis on craftsmanship renders it more like medieval building than modern. "You can't have both speed and craftsmanship; patience is of the essence," he said. Also, members should not hope for too much savings from standardization. He made the perceptive point that standardization is incompatible with individuality, and hence promises only limited benefit. Members were not getting cheap houses, but they were getting Usonian houses cheaper than they could get them anywhere else, and through a system available only through a cooperative organization.

Chuckrow hoped that Usonia would continue with him. But it was becoming clear that savings that may have been achieved through group construction were more than offset by the difficulties of accounting and allocation. There were not groups of houses to build simultaneously, but ones and twos and often interrupted funding. Within a year after this report, Usonia terminated Chuckrow's general contract and contracted houses out individually—to Chuckrow and before long to other builders as well.

Architects of unconventional houses have often complained of excessive costs resulting from a builder's unfamiliarity with their systems. Harold Turner had been asked several times to take over building in Usonia, but was not prepared to do so. At about this time David Henken, who had done some work on his own and relatives' homes, and thinking that Usonian designs could be built more efficiently, decided to be a builder. Operating from an addition to his home, he called his company "Henken Builds" and thereafter was the builder of most of his own designs as well as the Reisley House and, partly with Harold Turner, the Serlin House.

FINANCING AT LAST

In the summer of 1949, with five homes occupied and seven others nearing completion, Usonia still had no mortgage financing. What had been a serious problem was now becoming desperate. Some members dropped out, while others anxious to start building could not. Some short-term loans from banks and individuals were coming due. Priscilla Henken and Mildred Resnick each lent their husbands several thousand dollars to help the Design Panel pay its bills. Herb Brandon obtained a loan from a reputed Mafia figure who, it was said, threatened him with a "cement overcoat" if he was not repaid on time.

Over the years every member's lawyer, accountant, and family had been asked for bank suggestions. A number of institutions showed interest including Bowery Savings Bank, Metropolitan Life, Ohio Farm Bureau, Home Savings Bank, the Amalgamated Bank, First Federal

Savings and Loan, and others. The finance committee, which included Herb Brandon, Sol Friedman, Ralph Miller, and Rowland Watts, pursued these leads intensively but finally to no avail. Several banks indicated interest in giving mortgages, but only if the homes were individually owned. A growing number of members believed that choice was inevitable. A majority that included the active founders, however, was determined to keep trying for a group policy.

During much of 1949, however, one potential source was particularly encouraging. A section of the Federal Housing Administration (FHA) was committed to help cooperative and low-cost housing projects obtain financing. Ed Serlin, with his many media contacts, arranged a meeting between Thomas Grey of the FHA co-op division and himself, Herb Brandon, and Ralph Miller. Serlin also met the FHA publicity director and through him the secretary to U.S. Senator Flanders, then chairman of the Senate Banking Committee. Both described active interest in cooperatives and offered to help.

In the ensuing months members were kept informed of meetings with FHA representatives in Washington and New York. Applications and detailed financial data were prepared, revised, and discussed. At this critical juncture members felt that financing was imminent. Near the end of October Usonian Rowland Watts, who had been at the center of negotiations with the FHA, was told by Grey that Usonia's housing cost and monthly rents exceeded the FHA low-cost threshold for priority attention. Usonia could file its application, but it would likely be tabled.

Greatly disappointed, Usonia felt it had no choice, but to pursue a conventional mortgage. A number of mortgage brokers assured Usonia success if given exclusive representation and a contingent fee. Several were engaged but they did not succeed. The change to individual ownership loomed ominously.

In the middle of November Sol Friedman told the board of directors that he had met with the Knickerbocker Federal Savings and Loan Association and received a favorable reception, and that its appraisers would visit the land on November 28. The bank questioned the circular sites and asked for rectangles. Whether to satisfy the title company or the town, its surveyors claimed they could not manage the legal filing of circles. In fact they could have, but it would have been a bit more difficult and Usonia was in no position to insist. David Henken discussed the problem with Judge Kenyon, suggesting hexagons or polygons over the circles, for which she would write acceptable descriptions. Working with Henken, Aaron Resnick did much of the drawing, and Henken soon presented the plan with "hexed circles." Usonia intended, however, that the actual building sites remain circles.

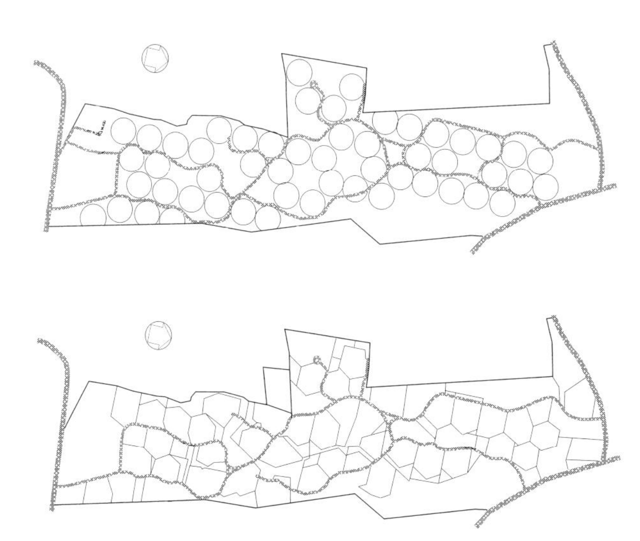

THE BANK AND TOWN OBJECTED TO FILING CIRCULAR SITES, SO THEY WERE FORMALLY FILED AS POLYGONS.

THESE DRAWINGS FROM THE FRANK LLOYD WRIGHT COMPANION *(UNIVERSITY OF CHICAGO PRESS, 1993) WERE PREPARED BY WILLIAM ALLIN STORRER, TO WHOM ALL USE RIGHTS BELONG. THE "AS DESIGNED PLAN" WAS DRAWN UNDER LICENSE FROM THE FRANK LLOYD WRIGHT FOUNDATION. COPYRIGHT © 1993.*

HOUSES DESIGNED BY KANEJI DOMOTO
clockwise from top left: HARRIS HOUSE, 1949
WALTER A. SLATTERY; CONSTRUCTION VIEW OF
LURIE HOUSE, 1949 *WALTER A. SLATTERY*; FINISHED
FRONT FACADE OF LURIE HOUSE

opposite: DAVID HENKEN HOUSE, 1949
top: CONSTRUCTION VIEW OF SOUTH FACADE
WALTER A. SLATTERY
bottom: LIVING ROOM *© PEDRO E. GUERRERO*

"WE ARE BANKING ON THE FUTURE, NOT THE PAST....HERE WE HAVE A GROUP THAT IS SETTING A NEW PACE BOTH IN COOPERATIVE OWNERSHIP AND ARCHITECTURAL DESIGN." LOUIS T. BOECHER, PRESIDENT OF KNICKERBOCKER FEDERAL SAVINGS AND LOAN

Soon Usonia's directors met with Knickerbocker's board of directors. Two homes and two sets of plans were appraised and the bank offered four and three-quarters percent mortgages on sixty percent of estimated cost. Twelve more applications were being processed. Knickerbocker was willing to grant mortgages if individual owners would cosign the loan. Knickerbocker appraisers toured the construction site and indicated satisfaction with the quality and design of the houses. Evidently, they were also impressed by the architecture and the association with Frank Lloyd Wright. Louis T. Boecher, president of Knickerbocker, quoted in *Architectural Forum* and other media, said:

> Here we have houses designed by Mr. Wright himself, and, as usual, twenty to thirty years ahead of their time. At the tag end of these loans we will be secured by marketable, contemporary homes instead of dated stereotypes, obsolete before they are started. We are banking on the future, not the past.... Here we have a group that is setting a new pace both in cooperative ownership and architectural design.
>
> We think this will become an increasingly significant form of home ownership. We like it because we think group developments offer both the lender and the owner the maximum of protection against the greatest single factor in realty depreciation—that of neighborhood deterioration.

Although Boecher's prediction about cooperative ownership would not be borne out, he was quite correct about the neighborhood appreciating, which it has done more than thirty-fold on the average since 1950.

Knickerbocker ultimately agreed to give Usonia a mortgage, but only after a complicated—even brilliant—proposal had been worked out by Dorothy Kenyon. In his book, *Frank Lloyd Wright: His Life and His Architecture*, Robert C. Twombly noted that under Kenyon's scheme the bank and the cooperative (and the cooperative and its members) struck up a highly creative relationship. Knickerbocker Federal Savings and Loan Association agreed to give the cooperative a four and three-quarter percent (one quarter percent over the normal rate), ten- to twenty-year group mortgage. All houses would be used as security, including those already built and paid for. Usonia would hold title to all the land and houses. Members would pay rent monthly to amortize the mortgage and meet community expenses. They would also go on bond personally for their own ninety-nine-year leaseholds, which could be passed on to heirs. If Usonia defaulted for any reason, individual members would be responsible for the mortgage on their own houses and land. If members experienced financial difficulty, the cooperative was empowered to carry them for at least six months. Members wishing to withdraw from the community would turn their houses over to Usonia for sale. If the house were sold at a profit, withdrawing members would take away any built-up equity plus their share in the profits. (This share would be determined by the inflation index of the U.S. Bureau of Labor Statistics.) If the house sold at a loss, however, the withdrawing member would have to absorb the difference.

Usonia was now the main mortgagee; members paid rent to the cooperative rather than to the bank. Rent included interest and amortization of mortgage, taxes, and an equal share of community expenses. Mortgages were based on the bank's appraisal, not on the cost of the house or the member's investment. From Usonia's beginning members knew they were expected to have forty percent of the anticipated cost of their house in an account with Usonia, and that the balance would be mortgaged. But, as costs exceeded estimates, some were unable to come up with forty percent.

To raise needed funds Usonia sought the largest mortgages it could get, even if the amount was more than the individual member needed to build his or her house. This set up a complicated but workable scheme in which members were compensated for these larger-than-needed mortgages. Sometimes the opposite was true: members were unable to get a large enough mortgage, in which case Usonia stepped in to fill the gap. Thus, on Usonia's books at various times, some members were listed as over-mortgaged and others under-mortgaged. The cooperative could also extend protection to members in difficulty, preserving the all-for-one spirit of the enterprise.

Now that mortgage money was at last within reach, a thorny problem remained: To determine the individual costs of the first five houses, which were built with the community's pooled resources. Forty thousand dollars of expenditures had to be allocated between the houses and Usonia. But just how? Several committees pored over the records, such as they were, trying to estimate the relative amounts of labor and materials in the homes and, after much debate, allocated $14,000 to be charged among the owners of the first five houses proportionately. The rest was considered to be Usonia development costs. The committees' decision was adopted but never really accepted by some members, who thought that they, Usonia, were paying more than they should have for other members' homes. Usonians' optimism was tempered by the reality that being part of a cooperative often required compromise.

Knickerbocker's agreement to provide mortgages greatly relieved and energized the Usonians. Some were settling into their homes and becoming acquainted with the neighborhood. More homes were completed and others started. And after years of planning members could actually live together as close neighbors in their own homes and their own community.

DESPITE OBSTACLES, BUILDING CONTINUES

Though the land had been acquired, houses had been occupied, and mortgages had been obtained, the board of directors continued to meet weekly in homes in Pleasantville or Manhattan, usually with other members sitting in. The minutes of those meetings (more than one hundred meetings in 1950 and 1951 alone) included matters of design, membership, and community activities, but they were mostly dominated by cost of construction and financial issues. Although each home was designed for an individual member who would ultimately pay for it, clearly Usonia was the builder. The board, which had to authorize all payments, was concerned with the performance of work and its cost despite supervision by the architects, the Design Panel,

PODELL HOUSE, 1949, BY DAVID HENKEN
left: CONCRETE BLOCK WALLS WERE "CORBELLED" (OFFSET TO NARROW FROM TOP TO BOTTOM). WHEN WET, WATER DRIPS FROM THE EDGE OF THE BLOCKS, RATHER THAN ALONG THE WALL. THIS ALSO CREATES A DECORATIVE DETAIL.
right: THE INTERIOR SHOWS HENKEN'S USE OF SHELVES APPEARING TO CONTINUE THROUGH GLASS. HE OFTEN MADE PLANTERS IN FLOOR SLABS WITH GLASS SEPARATING INSIDE FROM OUTSIDE, EMULATING WRIGHT'S SIMILAR DEVICES.

and the contractor. Because more members now lived in Usonia, the board ordered new stationery with the Pleasantville address, stipulating that it carry a union label. The clerk of the works, Murray Smith, was authorized to set up an office in the Quonset hut in Usonia. The post office did not deliver along the unpaved roads so a row of mailboxes grew at the northern end of Usonia Road.

The houses belonged to Usonia and Usonians felt a proprietary interest in each of them. For many members that sense of the cooperative's interest had a unifying social and psychological impact. During construction members strolled freely through each other's homes and, when guiding a visitor, would proudly describe the architectural features. Years later, most members still felt a comfortable familiarity with the homes of their neighbors in Usonia.

But the community had one more obstacle to hurdle. The local architects' association, not very sympathetic with the designs they saw, learned that the Mount Pleasant building department was rather casually approving Usonia's "radical" buildings, including some by architects who were not licensed or not licensed in New York. They complained to the New York State Board of Regents, which in turn demanded and received assurance of Usonia's future compliance. This was not a small matter for it revealed that David Henken was not a licensed architect. (Henken, an industrial engineer, learned about architecture as a Wright apprentice at Taliesin. Wright believed that was the best way to learn and he disapproved of formal architectural training.) Thereafter, Henken's designs were reviewed and stamped by an architect friend, Joseph Saravis.

At about the same time the building inspector of the town of Mount Pleasant, now alerted to the licensure requirement, refused to issue a building permit for the Wright-designed Serlin House, saying that the plans were not stamped by a New York licensed architect. Serlin may have been the only member to join specifically seeking a home designed by Frank Lloyd Wright. Serlin sprang into action, telling the inspector of Wright's world-famous buildings, including those in New York—in Buffalo, Rochester, and Great Neck. He also arranged for a representative of the state Department of Education to visit Wright, who was in New York, to explain the application procedure. To expedite the process Serlin exchanged numerous letters and phone calls with Wright and the bureaucracy involved, which culminated in his authorization to order and pick up an official New York State seal for Frank Lloyd Wright, license number 6239.

Henken's lack of a license however precipitated other events. The Design Panel, a partnership of Henken and Resnick, was legally responsible for architectural work in Usonia. The panel was then in contention with Usonia and several individual members on a variety of issues, and a committee was actively exploring revisions to the panel's functions and contract. Resnick received legal advice to end the Design Panel contract and his partnership with Henken. Issues related to the Design Panel and to Henken were seen differently among the membership and would contribute to the stressful polarization that lay ahead.

Yet, by the end of 1949 seven more homes were occupied: Ben and Frieda Henken moved in on August 12. The house designed by their son, David, was a nine-hundred-square-foot gem featured in many news stories on Usonia. Next came Odif and Judeth Podell on September 2, David and Priscilla Henken on October 2, Herbert and Ada Brandon on October 22, Arthur and Gertrude Bier on December 15, and Bill and Esther Harris on December 23.

The Friedman, Victor, and Wax houses followed in the fall of 1950. Priscilla Henken wasted no time in reporting on her family's experience. In a letter to Wright's secretary Gene Masselink, on October 6, 1949, she wrote enthusiastically: "We have finally moved into our Usonian home. Moved into is a euphemism—outside of would be more correct.... Our wild life at present consists of cows, deer, squirrels, and children. Good though."

After five years of dreaming, planning, and struggle, there were twelve homes, more on the way, and financing available.

A CRACK IN THE FOUNDATION

There were many pressures still facing the community. Although mortgage money was now at hand, there was still a need for more new members. In meetings with prospective members, Usonians emphasized the core principles of the community: adherence to Wright's philosophy of design, acceptance of a true cooperative structure, and affordable housing achieved through innovative design and cooperative construction.

Initially, admission to Usonia required clear acceptance of these principles, especially during the exciting years of planning and education. But gradually, this rigid insistence relaxed as building began and financial pressures grew. Acceptance of these ideals, all viewed as benefits, could not obscure the member's considerable risk, particularly the financial exposure and problems that might erupt from making a long-term commitment to living with a group in the country.

Many later members recall that they were especially attracted to Usonia by the enthusiastic commitment of the members who preceded them. The risks seemed more acceptable "if we were all in the same boat." The founders and early members attracted others who, for the most part, shared their views. But by 1950 the much higher than expected construction costs and urgent need for new members led a few Usonians to reexamine their commitment to the community's core principles. Not only did the high architectural standards add to the cost, but delays in seeking Wright's approval only seemed to aggravate the situation. The co-op structure itself and limited access to financing also deterred some prospective members. Though the majority was determined to continue as planned, it was becoming clear that under financial pressure members' priorities varied. For some, the highest concern was the social philosophy of a cooperative community; for others it was the "organic" architecture; for one or two, it was mainly affordability that counted; for most it was some combination of these. Eventually their differences became a divisive issue, as a rift developed between those who wished to preserve the founding "credo" ran up against those who became more concerned with financial issues.

Usonians had their hands full finishing their homes, discovering their actual cost, calculating and collecting rents, and trying to decide how to proceed more efficiently. Chastened by much higher than expected building costs, the board and individual member's efforts focused on ways to more accurately estimate and control the cost of their not-yet-built homes.

BRANDON HOUSE, 1949, BY DAVID HENKEN
clockwise from top left: EXTERIOR VIEW INCLUDES LIVING ROOM AND PLAYROOM EXTENSIONS BY AARON RESNICK; INTERIOR VIEW OF KITCHEN AND REVISED DINING AREA; FLOOR PLAN. *REDRAWN BY TOBIAS GUGGENHEIMER STUDIO*

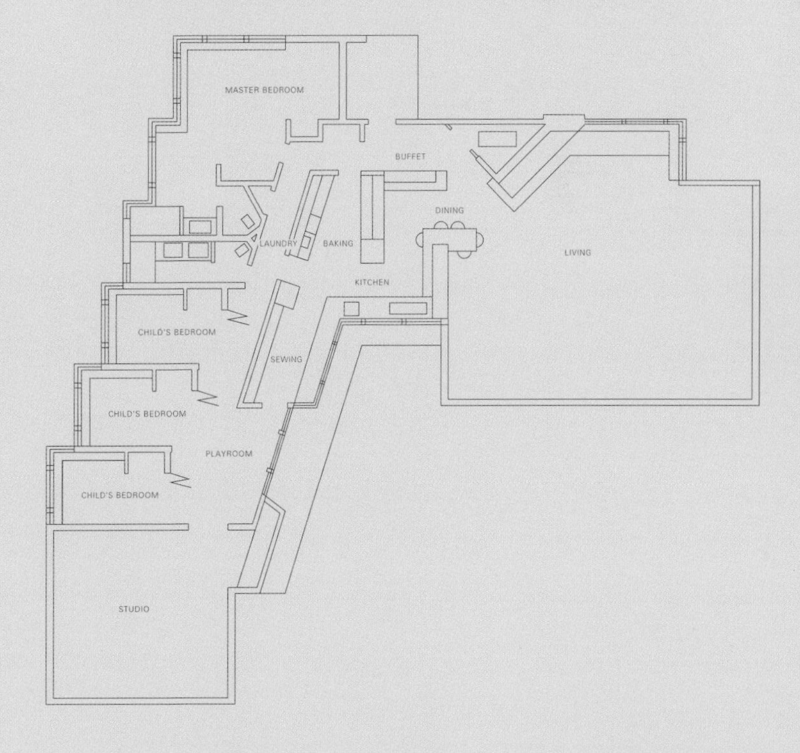

Chapter Five WORKING WITH FRANK LLOYD WRIGHT

FRANK LLOYD WRIGHT'S RELATIONSHIP WITH USONIA BEGAN WITH HEADY IDEALISM ON ALL SIDES AND ENDED IN DISAPPOINTMENT. HE WAS CLEARLY ENTHUSIASTIC ABOUT USONIA HOMES, WHICH PROMISED TO BE "A PIECE OF BROADACRE CITY," AS HENKEN AND OTHERS DESCRIBED IT. DESPITE BEING IN HIS EARLY EIGHTIES, AND DESPITE BEING BUSIER THAN EVER BEFORE IN HIS LONG CAREER, WRIGHT DEVELOPED THE SITE PLAN, DREW PLANS FOR A COMMUNITY CENTER, AND DESIGNED FIVE HOUSES FOR USONIA. THREE OF his original designs, the Friedman, Serlin, and Reisley houses, were built. Due mainly to concerns over cost, the houses he designed for Sid and Barbara (Bobbie) Miller and Irwin and Ottalie Auerbach and the community center never materialized. Forty of the forty-seven houses in Usonia were designed by Wright and his former apprentices or disciples, while two of the other seven homes were later remodeled by Wright apprentices.

When critical of a design Wright would shoot off an exasperated, even caustic, letter, as a 1949 exchange with Ted Bower shows. Bower, a former Wright apprentice, was dispatched by Taliesin to oversee construction of Wright's Friedman House. He also designed a few of his own. Commenting on Bower's preliminary sketches for the Scheinbaum House, Wright wrote:

> Dear Ted,
>
> Your disconnected opus—-a nightmarish abuse of privilege—is at hand.... Try again and don't take originality at any cost as an objective... don't make game of your sojourn at Taliesin. Try to do something free from such affectation.
>
> Sincerely,
>
> Frank Lloyd Wright

As if that were not damning enough, Wright later told Bower that the low concrete dome on the roof looked like "a bald pate with excema." Bower, known to be a little confrontational himself, replied, "I could do without the sarcasm that was smeared so thick over your criticism." However, accepting Wright's comments, he added, "I think the faults of the design were out of awkwardness, not affectation. I wanted to use the dome form not only

FRANK LLOYD WRIGHT REVIEWING A BUILDING DESIGN WITH SOL FRIEDMAN (CENTER) AND DAVID HENKEN (RIGHT).

HENRY RAPISARDA, COSMO-SILEO ASSOCIATES

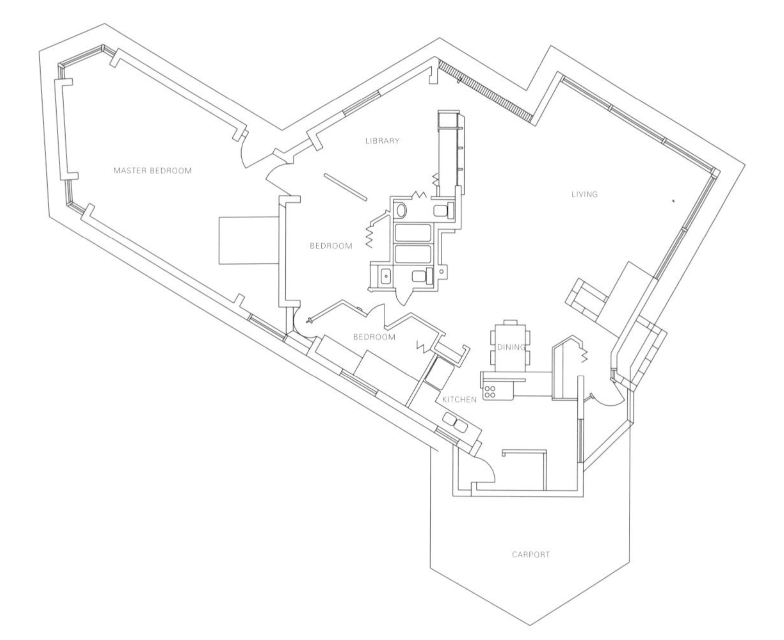

SCHEINBAUM HOUSE, 1951, BY TED BOWER

clockwise from top left: BOWER USED ROSE-TINTED CONCRETE BLOCK, NATURAL REDWOOD FASCIA AND MILLWORK, AND A RED-SHINGLED DOME ROOF. LATER ADDITIONS BY DAVID HENKEN INCLUDED NEW BEDROOMS (LEFT) AND ENLARGED THE LIVING ROOM (RIGHT); INTERIOR VIEW SHOWING LIVING ROOM, DINING ROOM, AND ENTRY; FLOOR PLAN. *REDRAWN BY TOBIAS GUGGENHEIMER STUDIO*

because it seemed appropriate to the site but also because it seemed possible to economize by spanning the house with an arched shell instead of a flat heavily reinforced slab. I am interested not in novel effects but in integrity."

He redrew the house according to Wright's suggestions, explaining, "The roof shell is not to be bone-white but a light earth-red, just dark enough and colorful enough to take well the mellowing effect of the weather." The house was a tiny hexagon. Seen from the road, the red shingled dome surrounded by white gravel, all encircled with a red fascia, became an iconic image. Ted recalled a female member of the co-op saying, "that roof practically gives me an orgasm every time I go by it!"

Although Wright occasionally dealt directly with Usonia's architects and clients, his main channel of communication with the community was David Henken. Wright knew David and saw him not only as Usonia's founder but also its leader. Henken also thought his role as Usonia's designated intermediary was appropriate and necessary, as did most Usonians. Henken's contract—originally through the building committee, then the architectural association, and finally through the Design Panel—formalized this role. Thus, apart from Wright's visits to the community, Usonians usually heard his decisions and opinions from Henken. These commentaries will be explored later in the chapter, but first the homes Wright designed himself will be explored

THE FRIEDMAN HOUSE

In February 1948 Sol and Bert Friedman asked Frank Lloyd Wright to be their architect. The Friedmans had little knowledge of architects when they joined the cooperative and perhaps chose Wright because he was regarded as "the best." Their $30,000 budget, in 1948, was substantial—two or three times that of most other members. Sol Friedman was a successful retailer, mainly in college bookstores, though some of his stores also sold toys and records. Wright seized upon the idea of Friedman as a toy maker—even though he was not—and intended the fanciful, circular design of the Friedman House to reflect that occupation. Wright dubbed the house "Toyhill," but the name was rarely used.

The Friedman House is the best known of the Wright houses in Usonia. Like the community's serpentine roads and circular plots, the house reflected Wright's growing interest in the circle as a basis of design. Two overlapping cylinders comprise the structure. The larger cylinder is two stories high and includes the Usonian core: a generous living/dining/workspace area, with large curving windows that give broad views of the outside. The smaller cylinder provides wedge-shaped bedrooms and baths on one side and on the other a cantilevered balcony/playroom projecting over the main living space. A spiral staircase at the masonry core connects the two stories. Each cylinder has a circular roof with Wright's characteristic overhanging eaves. A long stone wall runs from the entrance to a distinctive carport composed of a large disc supported by a central stem.

The house is built mainly of concrete and local stone. From the outside it suggests a fortress on a promontory. Inside, the curving living space gives a sense not only of movement, but also of connection to the outside, as from a tree house floating in a forest. Like so many of Wright's designs, the Friedman House combines communion with the surroundings with a definite sense of privacy.

The working drawings for the house arrived in the spring of 1949. Wright apprentice Ted Bower supervised

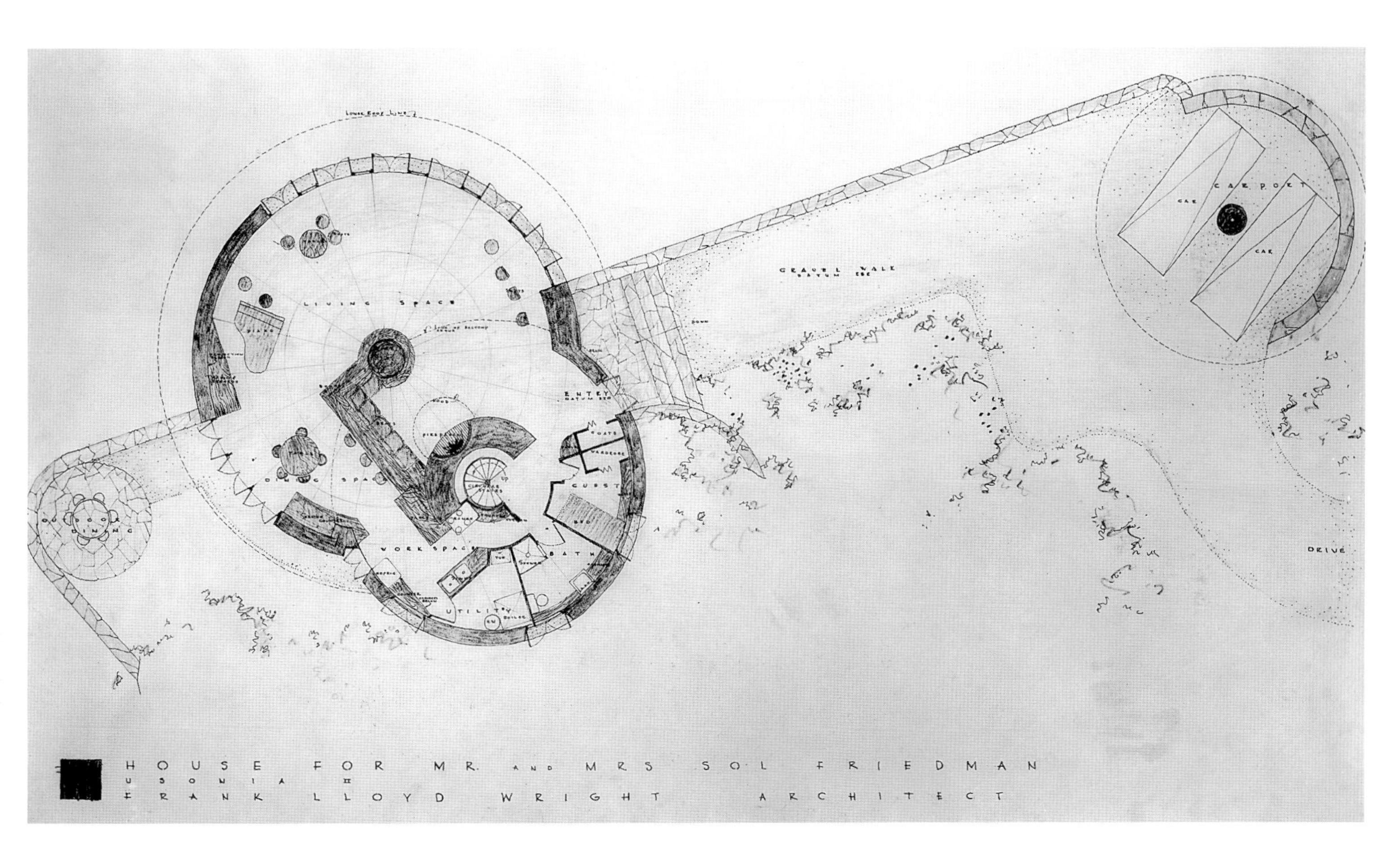

opposite: ON-SITE DISCUSSION, (FROM LEFT) TED BOWER, ROBERT CHUCKROW, FRANK LLOYD WRIGHT, UNIDENTIFIED MAN, AARON RESNICK, DAVID HENKEN, AND SOL FRIEDMAN. BOWER WAS WRIGHT'S ON-SITE SUPERVISOR FOR BUILDING THE FRIEDMAN HOUSE. *HENRY RAPISARDA, COSMO-SILEO ASSOCIATES*

above: RENDERING OF FLOOR PLAN FOR FRIEDMAN HOUSE, 1950, BY FRANK LLOYD WRIGHT. *COURTESY THE FRANK LLOYD WRIGHT FOUNDATION, SCOTTSDALE, AZ*

top: DINING TERRACE (LEFT) AND "MUSHROOM" CARPORT (FAR RIGHT) OF THE FRIEDMAN HOUSE.
bottom: NIGHT VIEW.

its construction, which quickly escalated into costly budget overruns. The extremely innovative nature of Wright's design required many on-the-spot interpretations that Bower found difficult, even after four years at Taliesin. On top of that, the topographical survey from which Wright worked was inaccurate, so the building had to be moved farther from the road to comply with local zoning. Bower began an extensive series of communications with Wright in which he proposed a number of solutions, many of which Wright accepted. At times Bower complained that Wright's senior apprentices gave inadequate replies. Bower could be testy and demanded clarification, which led Wright to chide him with what Bower later called "Olympian sarcasm."

> Dear Ted:
>
> . . . Now, you are a very remarkable young man, no doubt, who stumbled into Taliesin to enable me to improve upon myself greatly and I am thankful as a matter of course.
>
> And yet the validity of my own experience still seems precious to me where buildings are concerned. You should not blame me for this.
>
> "A spoon may lie in the soup for a thousand years and never know the flavor of the soup"—but that is always the other fellow—never us as you yourself may learn sometime. . . .
>
> So I should say you—Ted—need a fair dose of either a spiritual emetic or cathartic to evacuate an over-heavy charge of Ted and clear up our way ahead considerably at this junction of our lives.
>
> What do you think.
>
> Affection,
>
> Frank Lloyd Wright

Complications with construction continued. When the conical ceiling framing of sixteen-foot-long two-by-fours was nearly complete, Bower realized the framing—which resembled the spokes on an umbrella—was beginning to sag. He suggested tripling the two-by-fours and Wright agreed. To save weight and money Wright changed the ceiling covering to sheet rock sprayed with a textured stucco-like material to match the concrete on the rest of the house. He also changed the living room windows, which had been a horizontal band, adding concave circular arcs under some of them to emphasize the circular character of the house. Those changes, the complicated detailing, and other alterations—some aesthetic, some structural, but all costly—took the house from a starting point of around $30,000 to a stunning $80,000!

The house became one of Wright's most highly regarded later designs. It was not only innovative but also in some ways radical. A round house with a circular roof and wedge-shaped rooms was certainly not the norm. A few people thought that the bedrooms were awkward and too small. Wright did urge the Friedmans to accept fewer bedrooms for their sons. "Double deckers are fun—our grandsons love them," he told them. Other people thought the spiral staircase was inappropriate for a house with small children. Indeed the bedrooms are small, yet they easily accommodate all the necessities: beds, desks, drawers, and closets. Throughout the house, beautifully finished accordion doors provide access to storage spaces without the intrusion of projecting doors. The Friedmans and their children seemed to enjoy the house immensely, as have the families of later occupants.

The story of Toyhill is part of the lore of Usonia. Even more than the roads or the site plan, this house seems

top: BALCONY PROJECTION OF THE UPPER LEVEL, USED AS A PLAYSPACE.
bottom: WRIGHT'S LIVING-DINING-WORKSPACE IS REALIZED HERE.

BOTH PHOTOS © ROLAND REISLEY, ASSISTED BY HOWARD MILLER

to confer the Wright imprimatur on the settlement. From its inception it has continued to draw the interest of architects, critics, and scholars. Completed in the fall 1950, it was beautifully documented by architectural photographer Ezra Stoller, and featured in stories about Usonia in *Architectural Forum,* the *New York Times,* and other papers and magazines. The publicity drew hundreds of visitors who were welcomed by Usonia. Most members felt some proprietary pride in this significant house. After all, it was collectively owned.

The Friedman House became the focus for many Usonian meetings and parties in the early years. The great circular living room was comfortable for just one or two people, but could accommodate one hundred as well. The Friedmans helped to organize and arrange concerts there by the Pleasantville Junior Philharmonic, a group of Usonia's children joined by a few others from neighboring towns. These events were particularly enjoyable since Usonia in the early 1950s was quite remote from social and entertainment activities (although there was a movie theater in Pleasantville). Television did not yet occupy much if any time, and Usonians relied on each other for social activity. Many gathered at the Friedman House on Monday evenings for group singing. Soon they invited Ludwig Sheffield, a Pleasantville music teacher and organist, to lead them and called themselves the Cantata Group. After more voices from nearby joined, they outgrew the Friedman House and moved to a church in Pleasantville. The Cantata Group has continued and thrived ever since, though few know of its origins.

But the Friedman House had some negative impacts, too. This was the first Wright-designed house to be built in Usonia, and its many changes, costly overruns, and exorbitant price sent reverberations throughout the community. Usonians were relying on Wright to design several houses and oversee the rest, but could he produce the affordable houses they hoped for and wanted? In retrospect, perhaps Wright should have reigned in the costs for the Friedman House. But his estimates were based on his understanding of going prices in the Midwest, which often varied from what local (eastern) builders and contractors understood. (At that time, Westchester County was the most expensive place to build in the country.) But confidence in Wright was severely shaken by the Friedman House and interest in commissioning designs from him dimmed.

THE SERLIN HOUSE AND THE REISLEY HOUSE

By contrast with the exuberant, demonstrative Friedman House, the Serlin House is truly within Wright's "classical" Usonian mode. The low-built house is simple but elegant, accented by an upward-sloping roof. Trademarks of other Usonian-style houses are here: a gallery leads into the bedrooms and a lovely combined living/dining/workspace area features generous windows and a huge stone fireplace. The roof sweeps out over expansive windows and doors, which open to a broad terrace and the woods beyond. As with the Friedman and Reisley houses, local stone is well in evidence.

Ed Serlin asked Harold Turner and Ted Bower to build the house. They started the construction but their access to local building trades was limited. Before long David Henken, through his company Henken Builds, was brought in to complete it. Cost overruns were not as severe as those with the Friedman House, but the Serlin House also cost more than was projected. Wright's designs for future additions were not built, though years later Aaron

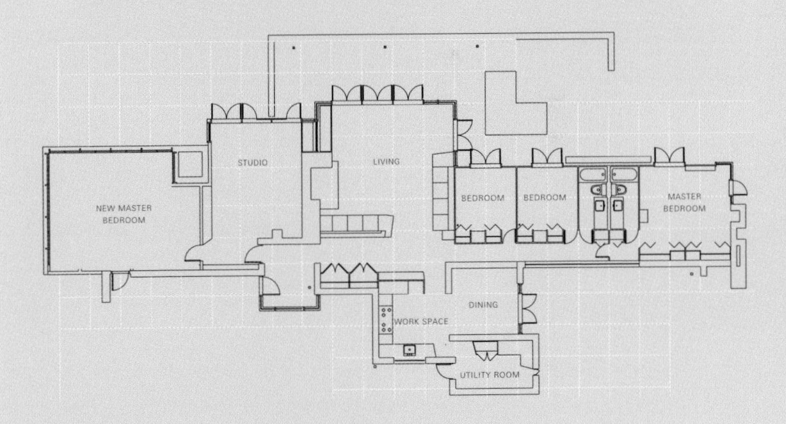

left: WRIGHT, WITH ED SERLIN, VIEWING "TOPO" OF SERLIN'S CIRCULAR SITE. *COSMO-SILEO ASSOCIATES*

top right: ED SERLIN AT THE DINING TERRACE OF HIS NEWLY COMPLETED HOME. *COURTESY THE SERLIN FAMILY*

bottom right: FLOOR PLAN OF THE SERLIN HOUSE. THE NEW MASTER BEDROOM WAS ADDED IN 1996 BY TOBIAS GUGGENHEIMER. *REDRAWN BY TOBIAS GUGGENHEIMER STUDIO*

top: SERLIN HOUSE FRONT TERRACE.
bottom: SERLIN HOUSE LIVING ROOM FACING DINING AREA.

Resnick modified what was to be a sculpture studio into a study for a new owner. The addition is seamless with the original.

The Serlins enjoyed cordial relations with Wright, and loved what he had designed for them. The house's relative simplicity compared to the other two Wright houses occasioned some good-natured jesting. Ed Serlin is supposed to have half-complained to Wright, "How come you gave the other houses these wild geometric designs, and all I get is this rectangle?" Wright replied grandly, "What are you complaining about? You got the fundamentalia."

The Reisley House, home of the author of this book, was the last of the three Wright houses to be built at Usonia. Set into a hill and seeming to grow from a huge boulder, the stone and cypress house has the long, low aspect that Wright championed. A fine example of a house truly becoming one with its surroundings, it shows Wright's facility in integrating a building with challenging terrain. The Reisleys' personal story of building their the house with Frank Lloyd Wright is found in the epilog to this book.

THE MILLER HOUSE

One of the houses Wright designed, but was not built, was the Sidney and Bobbie Miller house. In September 1948 the Millers chose Wright to be their architect. "We were told to ask for a house that was less than what we were willing to pay for because he would undoubtedly run over," Bobbie Miller said. So, prepared to go as high as $22,000, the Millers asked for a house at $11,000.

Sidney Miller's letter to Wright was full of optimism. "We want you to be our architect," Miller wrote, calling it a "longstanding dream." The letter included their desire for a large living room, a den-guest corner, three bedrooms, and one bathroom, as well as a kitchen and laundry large enough for two to work in, a screened porch, and terrace. They also asked for space to hang a collection of paintings by Bobbie's sister. They indicated willingness to reduce bedroom size to maintain maximum height in the living room. In a postscript they said they admired the Friedman preliminary drawings, which they had just seen, and continued: "It is a great temptation to put more money at your disposal.... We feel the wiser course is to design the house with the limited amount before stated."

On his copy of the letter from the Millers, Wright wrote on the margin, "Wall space, Study off LR, one bath, screened terrace, storage, small bedrooms, Veg and Fl garden." And he penciled a tiny sketch there: a "polliwog" hexagonal main room with narrow "tail" containing other rooms. Later, he wrote to Henken regarding the Miller's ceiling of $11,000, "There ain't no such animal. Fifteen thousand dollars is now the bottom for a good house. Might as well face it."

Wright drew three sets of plans for the Millers, which they considered very beautiful. Those plans reveal a house brilliantly suited to its site, with Usonian elements such as a large hexagonal living room, a wing of smaller rooms, a masonry core, and broad eaves. But price was still a large issue, and although Wright made some compromises to bring the price down—replacing stone with concrete block wherever possible, for example—the Millers were beginning to despair. Chuckrow had bid $28,000. The Millers thought that was too much and that the house would in fact cost much more. Wright's estimates reflected what he believed the house should cost. When the Millers

top: REISLEY HOUSE, 1952, BY FRANK LLOYD WRIGHT.
bottom: SIDNEY MILLER HOUSE, 1951, BY AARON RESNICK.

told him that local builders could not match his estimates, he sent Harold Turner, claiming, in Sid Miller's words, that "the local guys don't know what they're doing." Turner thought Chuckrow's bid reasonable, and that he, Turner, could build it for under $30,000 but would make no fixed bid. Still convinced that the house would cost more, the Millers protested that these bids exceeded their now-increased budget of $22,000.

Bobbie Miller was unhappy that Wright had not designed a larger kitchen with a window. If Wright were willing to make additional revisions it would take time. (Years later, Bobbie—recalling her experiences with Wright—said that she and her husband knew Wright liked large living rooms, so they asked for a smaller one with the extra space distributed to other rooms. Because Wright's design didn't reflect this, they felt he had disregarded their wishes. Perhaps in all the revisions, they forgot their original request to reduce the bedroom size to maintain the height of the living room.)

Practical considerations were now hurrying the Millers. Back in New York the lease on their apartment was running out. Postwar rent restrictions had kept rent down for middle-class renters, but Sid Miller's income had grown after the war to the point that soon the Millers would have to pay much higher rent. They felt it was time to have their own house, and very soon.

When the disappointed Millers approached Aaron Resnick for a design, he, in characteristically self-deprecating fashion, tried to dissuade them: "Thank you very much for thinking of me, but really, why don't you give Mr. Wright one more chance? A house by him will be much more beautiful than anything I could design and more valuable." By this time it was 1950, and the Millers had agreed to go as high as $28,000. In December 1950 they commissioned Resnick to design a house, which he did. They moved there in May 1951; it cost $31,000.

THE AUERBACH HOUSE

In 1950 Ottalie and Irwin Auerbach, devoted Wright aficionados, asked him to design their home. Wright proposed a spectacular house with a triangular theme. The Auerbachs requested a number of changes to the preliminary design, many of which Wright included in a set of working drawings.

The Auerbach budget was $15,000, but Chuckrow's bid came in at $23,500 ($21,500 with concrete block instead of brick). He warned that shortages due to the Korean War could drive the price even higher. Wright was upset when he heard the bid, and wrote to the Design Panel, via Henken, to voice his complaint: "Your estimate on the Auerbach is as phony as 'square foot' intelligence is apt to be," he raged. "Actually that house should not cost over $18,000. The enclosed space would then average about $20 per foot, which is $10 more than we pay in the Middle West." (Despite its severe impact on his clients, Wright's underestimation of the costs may be understandable. Should Wright, whose central interest was design, have been up-to-the-minute on the widely varied and rapidly changing building costs around the nation? Perhaps not.)

Wright suggested that working with builder Harold Turner, the house might be done with poured concrete and thus be cheaper. But Turner, after evaluating the situation, did not think that would reduce the cost. Finally, the Auerbachs asked Wright for a small Usonian Automatic. Composed of specially designed precast concrete

VICTOR HOUSE, 1951, BY AARON RESNICK. AFTER NEGOTIATIONS WITH FRANK LLOYD WRIGHT FELL THROUGH, THE AUERBACHS MODELED THEIR HOME AFTER THIS ONE.

top: VIEW OF FRONT FACADE. *© PEDRO E. GUERRERO*

bottom: VIEW OF LIVING ROOM. *JOSEPH W. MOLITOR*

blocks, Wright's Automatics were meant to be owner-built and thus cheaper. Later, Wright agreed to design one for the Auerbachs, but by then it was too late.

The Auerbachs felt they had no choice but seek another architect, and they asked Wright to release them. They had their eye on a simple yet handsome Usonian that Aaron Resnick had designed for Max and Trude Victor for a fixed bid by Chuckrow of $21,500. The Auerbachs asked the Usonia board if they could build the same house, which the board initially opposed. The Auerbachs then got Chuckrow to lower his price even further to $19,200 using less costly materials. The hitch was that the deal had to be accepted within two weeks. The Auerbachs pleaded their case and Resnick and the board reluctantly agreed.

THE REJECTION OF KANEJI (KAN) DOMOTO

Well before he worked on his own designs, Wright had reviewed and commented on perhaps a dozen houses proposed for Usonia as the consulting architect. The first drawings presented to Wright by the Design Panel were for houses designed by David Henken, Aaron Resnick, Paul Schweikher, and Kan Domoto. Nearly all of Wright's comments about these soon-to-be-built designs were cryptic and verbal. His few written comments were qualitative rather than architecturally specific. But Kan Domoto was singled out for his most severe treatment. At first Wright criticized, then ultimately rejected, Domoto's drawings. Domoto's clients, however, liked his plans and did not understand the rejection. This proved to be one of Usonia's most difficult problems.

Arthur and Gertrude Bier were the first to retain Domoto. He made his drawings and Wright hated them. In a letter to Henken, he noted, "Kan's designs are lousy—pretentious imitations. Ask him to do something simple." His letters made clear that he found Domoto's work derivative of his own, and he disliked the overtones of the International Style, which he called "Breuerism" (after architect Marcel Breuer) in Domoto's designs. (Ironically, Gertrude recalled growing up in Germany and dreaming to live someday in a Breuer house.)

Domoto's work was related to Wright's in several ways, most notably a use of Japanese motifs in a modern idiom. But Domoto had his own ideas about the use of materials, including vertical siding that Wright disliked. Wright rejected one set of Domoto plans three times, reportedly saying that "those roofs weren't designed by a roofer—they were designed by a draper." Each rejection and set of revisions caused delay and frustration for the family involved. Membership meetings were filled with debates over fairness and standards. (Today, Usonians recall the heated debates over horizontal versus vertical siding with amusement. But it was a real issue at the time: vertical siding was cheaper, but horizontal siding was clearly more appropriate in a Wrightian design.)

Part of the problem was that Wright did not give a detailed, flat-out blanket rejection of Domoto's work and, to a cooperative seeking some definitive word, that led to delays and exacerbated tensions. The board offered to pay Domoto's expenses to meet with Wright, but Wright was not anxious to see him. Finally, however, on learning that construction had started, Wright indicated changes to the designs and the Design Panel was authorized to make them. He wrote, "I further request that Usonia Homes do not claim nor imply that these rejected Domoto houses have my approval."

BIER HOUSE, 1949, BY KANEJI DOMOTO

top: VIEW OF MODEL. *COURTESY THE BIER FAMILY*

bottom: SIMILAR VIEW WHEN BUILT. *COURTESY THE BIER FAMILY*

left: VIEW OF BIER HOUSE WITH LATER EXTENSION, COMMISSIONED BY THE COOPER FAMILY, OF LIVING ROOM OVER BALCONY.
right: BIER HOUSE LIVING ROOM .
© ROLAND REISLEY, ASSISTED BY HOWARD MILLER

After several similar exchanges, however, Wright finally demanded Domoto's resignation and was encouraged in this by Resnick and Henken. They felt that Domoto was attracting clients by estimating unrealistically low costs. There was even confusion as to Domoto's status as a Wright apprentice. When Henken enlisted Domoto as a Usonia architect, he believed that Domoto had been an apprentice at Taliesin. Wright, however, claimed, "He was a gardener." The disagreement over Domoto's designs went on for months and strained Usonia's relationship with Wright as well as with several members, some of whom came to feel that Wright's approval was not essential and wanted to go ahead without it. Ultimately, five Domoto designs were built in Usonia. A few of his clients switched to other architects.

Wright seemed to take these problems personally, and began distancing himself from the cooperative. By early spring Wright seemed to have soured on the cooperative altogether. He felt his authority had been flouted, and on March 21, 1950, he shot off a letter that, instead of rejecting Domoto, appeared to reject Usonia:

> I've expressed my sentiments concerning your Kan Domoto sufficiently and finally. I do not feel it up to me to stick my nose in matters there further because it is your affair in the first place. I do not propose to assume any responsibility whatever for designs now building in the tract. My contribution will be only those houses I have planned and their original layout. Beyond that, I've no authority and now want none.

FRANK LLOYD WRIGHT AND THE DESIGN PANEL

Henken urged Wright to reconsider. "Through these trials," he wrote to Wright, "we have tried to remain steadfast to our ideals." He regretted that three of Domoto's houses "slipped by us into being" and promised that Usonia would not claim that Wright had approved Domoto's houses. He reminded Wright that the majority of the cooperative still wanted the close relationship with him. As virtually all communication to and from Wright came through Henken, he was caught in the middle, trying to put the best face on differing views. In so doing he lost the confidence of Wright and of many Usonians. The rift grew and signaled the beginning of the end for the Design Panel, along with significant changes within the community itself.

It is interesting to note that the arguments over the nature of Usonian architecture had reached this pass. There was something to the notion that what Wright was now calling "Usonian" was different from what he had been designing in the 1936–41 period. His prewar houses had been consistent in design and materials, and these were the houses that inspired the very first members of Usonia to dream that a Wright-led cooperative might be possible. Clearly, there had been a distinct change in Wright's designs after the war. His twenty or so prewar Usonian houses did indeed have a structural simplicity related to minimizing their cost. But Wright perhaps felt he had exhausted the idiom and wanted to do other things. The postwar Usonians were more complex, involving somewhat more complicated, exploratory design and use of materials.

Henken did his best to revive relations with Wright, describing Usonia as "a tender plant sprouting in

WRIGHT WOULD NOT BE DRAWN BACK. HE WROTE: "WHAT CAN I ADD TO WHAT I'VE ALREADY SAID TO EVERY MEMBER OF YOUR COOPERATIVE OF LETTING GREEN AMATEURS PRACTICING ARCHITECTURE...BUILD HOUSES IN USONIA HOMES, I DON'T KNOW."

large part from your ideas.... If we fail now, the resulting heartbreak would not only be painful in itself but would serve as an active deterrent to other groups who watch us from all over the nation.... With you, no matter how distant you are, we can forge ahead. Without you, any architect, Philip Johnson up or down, becomes the authority." Although he agreed that the Domoto problem was "not your affair," he closed the letter as he began, as student to master: "Usonia has been my own way of loving your work."

But Wright would not be drawn back. He wrote: "What can I add to what I've already said to every member of your cooperative of letting green amateurs practicing architecture (of whom Kan Domoto is most conspicuous) build houses in Usonia Homes, I don't know. Is there some financial advantage to these poor deluded people in getting half-baked imitations to live in? If so what is it?... It is already necessary to protect any connection I have with your people against this kind of graft."

Wright's rejection and other difficulties spelled the end for the Design Panel. A few months later Henken wrote to Wright, warning him of trouble ahead. "The Design Panel is on the way out. Led by Kan's clients in the main, and by those who are generally opposed to the cooperative. A long undercover campaign is bearing fruit." By August 1950 the Design Panel was defunct. With it ended Henken's formalized liaison with Wright in service of the community.

REGAINING WRIGHT'S APPROVAL

With the Design Panel dissolved, the board of directors sought to continue contact with Wright for review of proposed homes. On June 18, 1950, Jack Masson, President of Usonia, wrote to Wright. Citing Wright's contractual commitment to review Usonia's proposed designs, Masson asked him to acknowledge and reaffirm the agreement by signing at the bottom of the letter. Wright signed it, but also wrote, "AGREED, provided any judgement I may see fit to pass on the submission for approval is final and to be enforced by Usonia Homes, Inc."

A year later, in September 1951, the board wrote to Wright and asked for a definitive comment on a set of plans. Wright, not fully aware of the dissolution of the Design Panel, replied that Henken was to serve as sole liaison with him. Confirming the setting of Henken's star within the community, Herb Brandon, vice president of the board, informed Wright that the "Board of Directors cannot designate any sole person as the sole liaison with your office." It would, however, forward all plans to Wright and not assume approval without written notice.

In November 1951 Usonia asked Wright to approve plans for the Jack and Marge Robertson House. Intending to build it himself, Robertson had designed the house with some help from Henken. Wright called the plan "bad" with "no advantage taken of the site" and poor elevation. Was that a rejection, or a displeased acceptance? Again, it seemed as if Wright was unwilling to give a definitive thumbs-up or down. Ultimately, Henken made revisions that Wright approved and the house went forward.

In December Brandon wrote to Gene Masselink, Wright's secretary, about an invoice from Wright for payment of outstanding architect's fees on the Friedman, Miller, and Auerbach houses. The fees were based on building costs higher than the original budgets, but a good deal less than the actual costs. For example, for the Friedman House Wright asked for payment based on $67,000, not the $80,000 cost. And Wright asked for payment on the working drawings he produced for the Miller and Auerbach houses, as only partial payment for preliminary drawings had been made. "These bills came as a great surprise to us," Brandon wrote. "Usonia cannot assume responsibility in this matter," since the payments had been arranged via the Design Panel, dissolved since August 1, 1950.

Brandon's letter included notes from Sol Friedman, Sidney Miller, and Irwin Auerbach. Friedman said he had hoped for a house of $27,000 and had received something much more expensive. Miller wrote, "I recognize no financial liability for architect's fees as we were not provided with plans at anywhere near the specified cost figure agreed." He claimed that Wright had agreed to release him from his contract if he relinquished his building site so that the plans might later be offered to another member, in which case the architect's fee would be refunded to him. Irwin and Ottalie Auerbach wrote that Wright's original plans "were far too extensive and not specifically designed to meet our requirements."

top: ROBERTSON HOUSE, 1952. THOUGH ROBERTSON INTENDED TO BUILD IT HIMSELF, HIS DESIGN WAS REDONE BY DAVID HENKEN. LATER OWNERS HAVE MADE A NUMBER OF CHANGES.
bottom: HARRY MILLER HOUSE, 1952, BY GEORGE NEMENY.

It is impossible not to feel some sympathy for these members. All around them the custom-built houses were costing more than they thought they would. Wright tried to keep costs down, too, but design came first for him. Had these members contracted with Wright individually, they would undoubtedly have accepted their obligation to him. But in Usonia, working through the Design Panel and reinforced by some now-active members who felt that Wright and the Design Panel had treated them badly, their protest may be understandable.

Wright answered Brandon angrily. He insisted that he had not been working for the Design Panel, but for the individual members. "The work was done . . . for my clients. . . . My relation as architect was directly" with the Millers, Friedmans, and Auerbachs.

> I had not thought of releasing them from their obligation to me for work done. . . . I do not make plans for specified sums, but . . . do my best to serve [clients] according to my ability in the circumstances as they may appear. This I did for them. . . . Nothing for me to do now, I guess, but turn your cases over to my lawyer in Washington for collection and instruct him to file liens upon their house. If you are now operating the so-called Usonia Homes, it is high time for me to sever any connection I may have had with that project. I wish it well known that I never had any real connection with the enterprise, since this type of thinking and acting as you represent is now characteristic of it: an original accessible only if as cheap, or cheaper than an imitation . . . a cheap exploitation of my name and work by inexperienced aspirants, whatever the original intent may have been. . . . This does not apply to either Roland Reisley or Ed Serlin, as I do not believe they are in the class you represent.

Brandon wrote back to say that a "serious misunderstanding exists between us." He blamed the Design Panel: the "impressions you received from the Design Panel were not an accurate reflection of the situation as we understood it." He defended Miller and Auerbach, noting that the bids for their houses had been far in excess of Wright's estimates.

Something like a final break came when Wright wrote to Henken on January 30, 1952. He apparently believed that the Design Panel still existed and was clearly confused and tired of the whole matter: "I understand that I am . . . subject to the Design Panel who employ me and pay me when they get [the money] from my client . . . instead of the DP being subject to me. . . . With this rude awakening, I withdraw from this and any such equivocal situation as a 'sucked orange,' so to speak. I decline to consider or manifest either interest or responsibility for what plans are made for whom, wherever so-called Usonia Homes is concerned."

Nevertheless, Henken sent his new plans for the Robertson House to Wright in February 1952. He assured Wright that the Design Panel had been set up as a "convenience" for Usonia and that "whatever fees we have received for you have been forwarded to you promptly." Henken felt that the board of directors "hoped to make you angry enough to turn against me and withdraw from Usonia. . . . A sizable group of Usonians, as well as the bank, are on your side, so don't desert us." Henken again struck the note of devoted follower that characterized his dealings with Wright. Probably aware that the working relationship between Usonia and Wright was all but over, Henken reminded Wright that "I have dedicated myself to getting built as many of your designs as possible."

In February 1952 the board of directors urged Wright to comment on plans for the Robertson and Harry Miller houses, the latter designed by George Nemeny, who hoped to satisfy Wright, but whose work Wright disliked. Wright wrote back simply, "If you like these... build them. Usonia has nothing to lose." More wires from Usonia followed, one asking whether Wright had "decided to discontinue" the practice of review plans. Wright eventually did approve the Robertson plans, but his active era of commentary was over. When he and Henken next corresponded, it was to discuss the possibility that Henken Builds, the company Henken had created, could help construct the Usonian model house at the Frank Lloyd Wright exhibition pavilion that was erected on the site of the soon-to-be-built Guggenheim Museum. Wright said, "You can help," but not a word was exchanged about Usonia.

Wright began his association with Usonia as grand designer and overseer and ended frustrated, wishing to wash his hands of the whole enterprise. Usonia, Wright believed, had failed to live up to its pledge to create a truly organic community, bowing to pressures from amateurs and newcomers and thus letting in what he felt was inferior architecture. For their part some Usonians felt that Wright had not fully lived up to his side of the agreement—to design affordable modernist houses.

Yet by 1953 more than thirty houses had either been built or were in various stages of design or construction in Usonia, and Wright had had something to say about each one of them. And while his relationships with individual Usonians were not without storm and stress, most Usonians thought his comments and contributions were valuable and had improved their homes. Even when things were at their most stressful, the community still submitted drawings for Wright's comment and approval, in the hope that, even with the rocky course of recent events, he would continue to oversee Usonia's development. Clearly, his opinion and guidance were still important to them.

On Wright's part, even though at certain junctures he claimed to want nothing more to do with Usonia, he continued to comment on developments there well into the 1950s. In a sense he was committed, he could not let go: his name was associated with the community, had been widely published as such, and the community had used the association in publicizing itself. Wright helped the process along by speaking optimistically and hopefully about the community's progress. Despite his harsh words Wright stayed interested in Usonia. He was reluctant to sever all ties, as though holding out hope that Usonia could still become what he had hoped it would become.

Chapter Six REORGANIZING THE COOPERATIVE

USONIA CONTINUED TO GROW IN THE 1950S, BUT THE COOPERATIVE WAS NOT THRIVING AS HOPED. TENSION WAS BUILDING ALONG BOTH PHILOSOPHICAL AND FINANCIAL LINES. MONEY WAS CLEARLY THE ISSUE. EVERYTHING WAS COSTING TOO MUCH AND USONIA'S COMPLICATED FINANCIAL SYSTEM ONLY ADDED TO THE PROBLEMS. FIRST, NOT ONLY WERE THE COSTS OF LABOR AND MATERIALS RISING, BUT THE CHALLENGE OF BUILDING NEW, INNOVATIVE DESIGNS WITH INEXPERIENCED BUILDERS ALSO ADDED EXPENSE.

Usonians questioned the Design Panel's calculations and demanded justification of the amounts paid to their architects and the Design Panel. Second, the complexity of the cooperative acting as financial intermediary between individual members and their obligations to the bank, to the builders, and to the community resulted in a lack of confidence in the cooperative's efficiency and the accuracy of its figures. It also caused some corrosive disputes. Third, some members were unable to pay rent on time, which strained the community's very limited reserves and raised fears of jeopardizing relations with the bank. Knickerbocker Federal Savings and Loan Association, convinced that the poor condition of Usonia's unpaved roads deterred prospects, said it would not grant additional mortgages until the roads were improved. Without new members, Usonia's future was in serious jeopardy.

Either consciously or unconsciously, many Usonians realized that the community could not remain the same. Two factions thus emerged: those committed to Usonia's original founding principles and those who favored a massive organizational change. Some members felt that strict adherence to the Rochdale cooperative principles and the need to obtain Frank Lloyd Wright's approval discouraged new members and threatened Usonia's economic survival. Some feared financial instability and possible bank foreclosures if new members could not be found. But a larger, more vocal majority of true believers favored retaining the co-op's original ideals. Rather than face the charge of betraying principles to which they had agreed, the few members seeking change met quietly and privately. Their tactics however brought results. At the end of 1952 twenty-eight of the then thirty-

ZAIS HOUSE, 1955, TECH-BILT WITH LATER ADDITIONS BY MORTON DELSON AND OTHERS; ONE OF SEVERAL USONIAN HOMES BUILT AS THE COMMUNITY REDEFINED ITSELF

six members reluctantly supported the appointment of a committee "to investigate the possibilities of changing our financial structure." They wanted to retain the cooperative but consider transfer of the mortgage, title, and responsibility for each home site to the individual member.

The Usonians urging change wanted to protect not only their personal finances but also, they believed, Usonia itself. Even so, there was strong resistance to the idea of abandoning the cooperative. For some families, what had been Usonia's major attraction was now disappearing. "I was heartbroken," recalled Trude Victor, "because I, like everyone else, loved the cooperative. But I also knew we couldn't go on, things had to change."

The zeal of early members, most prominently David Henken, in defending the original structure and excoriating its critics was matched in intensity by a few of the proponents of change, the "revisionists," as they were called. These revisionists included Bill and Esther Harris and Jesse and Irene Lurie, who were original Domoto clients, as well as Herb Brandon and Sidney Miller, pragmatic businessmen who came to feel that cooperative ownership had hurt Usonia. Walter Tamlyn, who had just joined Usonia and felt called upon to "save Usonia from its and muddle-headed, fuzzy thinking self," was also in that group. An unresolved financial dispute with David Henken, over payment for his architectural work, seemed to reinforce their opposition to his views.

To explore the possibility of individual ownership required legal advice, but Judge Dorothy Kenyon, who had mentored and supported Usonia from its beginning, was not sympathetic to the revisionists. They then sought advice from another lawyer, Simon Sheib, and learned that a shift to individual ownership was not a simple matter. It would require rewriting the by-laws and abandoning the existing leases and subscription agreements that defined Usonia's commitments to its members.

Almost three years of tumultuous meetings—held several times a week and lasting for hours—followed. Usonians knew that unless the community's financial difficulties were resolved they could not get new mortgage loans and new members. On top of that, most of the members who had withdrawn from the community during the previous six or seven years had not been repaid their deposits and were now demanding return of their investments. Usonia owed a huge debt of $30,000, money the cooperative did not have.

At the same time David Henken sought payment of about $20,000 for outstanding fees and for consultation and construction on the first group of houses. After consulting with their new attorney, the board of directors determined that Henken was owed nothing further. Outraged, he withheld first his maintenance payments and dues, and then, in a final, telling stroke, his monthly mortgage payment to Usonia. (In fact, Henken was broke and soon forced into bankruptcy.)

Henken's refusal to make his payments exposed the vulnerability of the Rochdale Cooperative scheme, especially its all-for-one-and-one-for-all spirit. This only increased pressure to shift to individual ownership. A majority of Usonians now supported that change but other issues—the architectural standard, the sale of homes, and admission to membership—were now also on the table and hotly debated. Usonia's thirty-six families were divided roughly in thirds—one group opposed to change, another group in favor of change, and a third group whose views shifted depending on the issue.

clockwise from top left: TAMLYN HOUSE, 1953, BY AARON RESNICK; CARO HOUSE, 1956, BY AARON RESNICK; GRAYSON HOUSE, 1955, BY TOBIAS GOLDSTONE WITH LATER ADDITIONS BY AARON RESNICK; SCHEINER HOUSE, 1955, BY CHARLES WARNER.

clockwise from left: PARKER HOUSE, 1952, BY CHARLES WARNER, THE WIDER-THAN-ORIGINALLY-DESIGNED FASCIA WAS SUGGESTED BY FRANK LLOYD WRIGHT TO ADD "SOLIDITY"; BERMAN HOUSE, 1956, BY ULRICH FRANZEN, BORE THE WHITE, LINEAR SIMPLICITY OF HIS STYLE AT THE TIME, REMODELED BY CAROL KURTH IN THE 1990S; SIEGEL HOUSE, 1956, BY KANEJI DOMOTO.

Another change to Usonia's original structure was necessitated by the mid-1950s when Frank Lloyd Wright was no longer willing to review Usonians drawings. The community struggled to develop new wording for its by-laws that would maintain Wrightian architectural standards. They considered "shall be in accordance with the principles of Frank Lloyd Wright" and "shall be Usonian/organic architecture." But finally, after realizing that these "requirements" were not enforceable, members decided that new designs, or changes to existing structures, required approval of the board of directors. In a virtually unanimous (one no) vote, the membership directed that new members should be encouraged to select architects from Usonia's approved list.

Even Wright's site plan for Usonia came under renewed consideration. By 1955 the plan—which many Usonians regarded as the hallmark of the community—had been fully implemented. Although the home sites were legally filed as polygons, within the community they were still assumed to be circles. As physical delineation of boundaries (by fences, for example) was not permitted nor apparently desired, this was a rather subjective distinction, but it reflected Wright's view that the circles enhanced the sense of individuality within the larger wooded area. Some members, however, believed it was time to revise the plan to portion out the landlocked wedges between the circular sites, since they might be difficult to maintain. By increasing the area of each home site to 1.25 acres, Usonia could also eliminate some rights-of-way over community land for driveways. It would make some sites more attractive to new members, but also reduce the total number of sites from fifty to forty-seven. Seven families sued unsuccessfully to enjoin Usonia from altering the site plan. Nevertheless, the change was adopted. It was intended, though not required, that the original circle remain the building site.

After much debate the legal structure of the community was defined in 1955 in a set of restrictive covenants, renewable every twenty years. Any change would require 100% member approval—none has been made. The community adopted new by-laws to govern its operations. Member Sid Miller, a leader of the move to reorganize, observed: "We should do away with cooperative ownership of the houses.... Meanwhile, we can still really be a cooperative in all the ways that count. We own forty acres of community land, the roads, the water system. We depend on each other. We can still share things, do things together, still have community." Miller was correct, but the dispute over changes tended to isolate the earliest, founding group and their supporters. At many levels, however, the feelings of extended family prevailed, and the underlying polarization receded, albeit slowly.

By the middle of 1954 a board of directors committed to revision was in control of Usonia. Director Walter Tamlyn, an engineer of large industrial projects, was particularly active in those efforts. Before long he would become the president of Usonia, a position he held for many years. Tamlyn had some legal and financial perspective, and was the ultimate technocrat. He did much technical work on the roads and the water system. He would come out at night to repair the water pump, adjust the water chemistry, or help Usonians with mechanical problems at their homes. He also tended to various legalistic questions. He cared deeply for the community but had little interest in its esthetic ideals. "Frank Lloyd Wright was a nut," he asserted. Usonians often complained of his autocratic style, but they appreciated his work and accepted his style good-naturedly.

In 1955, by a close vote, Usonia Homes–A Cooperative, Inc. legally became Usonia Homes Incorporated. All members received deeds of ownership and shares of stock in the new cooperative. However all community land would be operated as a coop to which all member/owners must belong. They renewed their efforts to enroll the final eleven members to complete the community. Eight families joined by 1957 and the last three by 1963.

Arnold and Betty Zais were among the final eleven members to join Usonia. They became acquainted with the community when they rented the Sidney Benzer House in 1953 while Sid served as a U.S. Army dentist in Alaska. The Zaises learned about the impending change in Usonia's structure and hoped to join and support it. Asserting that their limited budget precluded a new Usonian design, they persuaded a reluctant Usonia to accept a Tech-Bilt design. These modernist, semi-pre-fab houses were designed by The Architects Collaborative, a firm associated with the International Style, which Wright was known to abhor. Sometime later the Zaises acknowledged that it was not simply economics that drove their decision. They preferred non-Usonian architecture and believed that Usonia should not insist upon Usonian houses.

With the architectural standards relaxed following reorganization, another Tech-Bilt was approved for Irving and Gloria Millman. Interestingly, both Tech-Bilts were later extensively remodeled by former Taliesin apprentices, one by Morton Delson and the other by David Henken, making them more in keeping with the rest of Usonia. The most noticeable departure from Usonian architecture, however, was the Stephen and Ellen Berman House designed by Ulrich Franzen. Essentially a white box on piers, it epitomized the style Frank Lloyd Wright taught Usonians to oppose and was facetiously described as "a beachhead of the enemy." But it was a perfectly fine house that could not "harm" Usonia, which by then was virtually complete.

Other new families built more typically Usonian houses. In 1955 Robert and Norma Siegel's lawyer, Simon Sheib, enthusiastically told them of Usonia, as it was about to be reorganized. They engaged Kaneji Domoto as their architect. Aaron Resnick's brother Sam and his wife Amy of course knew all about Usonia. They hired Aaron as their architect, and he designed a home that included some significant innovative design. The Martin and Jane Scheiner House was designed by Charles Warner, who also designed the Wright-reviewed Parker House. Its huge copper wall remains a prominent, familiar sight from Usonia Road.

It was much easier for the last families to build homes in Usonia, as they did not share the risks and many of the struggles of the earlier members. Ironically, however, Usonia seemed easier for the later members to leave. Seven of the last eleven chose to move on, whereas, of the earliest thirty-six members only four chose to leave, excepting cases of infirmity or death.

The painfully bitter and divisive reorganization was complete by the late 1950s and most of the "wounds" began to heal. As Sid Miller had predicted, Usonia continued to be a cooperative in many aspects. Usonia maintained its own water system, roads, community land, and recreation areas. A cycle of shared celebrations continued, as did the strong sense of a community with very much in common.

SAMUEL RESNICK HOUSE, 1958, BY AARON RESNICK.

Chapter Seven DAVID HENKEN: OUR MOSES

NO ONE WORKED HARDER TO MAKE USONIA A SUCCESS THAN DAVID HENKEN. IF FRANK LLOYD WRIGHT WAS USONIA'S GRAND DESIGNER AND OVERSEER, THEN HENKEN WAS ITS SPIRITUAL GODFATHER. HIS WHITE-HOT IDEALISM AND ENERGY DROVE THE GROUP. THE COMMUNITY HAD BEEN HIS DREAM SINCE THE LATE 1930S; HE STUDIED AND LABORED TO BRING IT INTO BEING FOR MORE THAN A DECADE. BUT AT THE VERY MOMENT WHEN HE WAS IN THE BEST POSITION TO ENACT HIS IDEAS, OTHERS CAME IN WITH DIFFERING GOALS that threatened his dream. After Henken initiated the idea of Usonia, he spent huge amounts of time gathering information from cooperatives, architects, builders, and manufacturers of materials. It would be several years before any actual design was needed, giving the community time to plan, learn, enroll members, and seek finance. Henken was a founding member of Usonia's board of directors. His father, Ben, was Usonia's treasurer; his sister, Judeth, the secretary and membership chair; and his brother-in-law, Odif, chairman of the education committee. Although it may have appeared otherwise, Henken was not "packing" the board; the membership was still quite small. His relatives were capable and anxious to serve but, amid suggestions of nepotism, he quickly withdrew from the board. He remained Usonia's de facto leader nevertheless.

Henken believed the cooperative should be an exemplary democracy, committed to the founding principles to which the members of Usonia had agreed. He also believed that he, as the founder, was in a better position than anyone else to interpret those principles. Perhaps he was right about that, but clashes of ego and personality led some members to resign from the community. Unable to proclaim authority, he tried to exercise some degree of control from behind the scenes.

Henken was the main conduit through which Usonians communicated with Wright, yet he ended up an outcast. All parties, it seems, felt cheated. Wright felt Usonia had failed to live up to its pledge to create a truly organic community, bowing to pressure from "amateurs" and "newcomers" and thus letting in what he felt were inferior styles. Some Usonians felt Wright had ignored

DAVID HENKEN REVIEWS DRAWINGS WITH FRANK LLOYD WRIGHT WHILE ROLAND REISLEY LOOKS ON *© PEDRO E. GUERRERO*

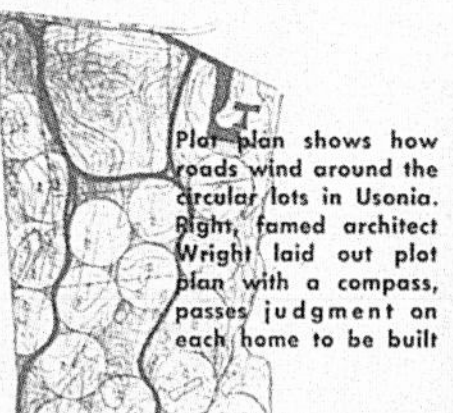

Plot plan shows how roads wind around the circular lots in Usonia. Right, famed architect Wright laid out plot plan with a compass, passes judgment on each home to be built

Cosmo Sileo photo

Fugitives from the city, these suburbanites put their piggy banks together to build a . . .

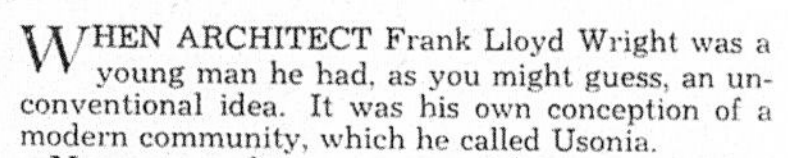

"CO-OP" VILLAGE in the WOODS

Walter A. Slattery photo

Most of the homes are low and solar-oriented. Roof trellises on this home by Henken will be covered with vines

By Clifford B. Hicks

WHEN ARCHITECT Frank Lloyd Wright was a young man he had, as you might guess, an unconventional idea. It was his own conception of a modern community, which he called Usonia.

Many years later, a successful young engineer named David Henken also had an idea. His was quite conventional. He wanted to build a home for his family.

Through a fortunate accident, Henken's idea smacked head-on into Wright's. The collision produced, not just a home for Henken, but perhaps the most unusual community in America.

It's a village that meanders all over a wooded, hilly tract near New York City. Its modern homes boast such unconventional features as circular lots, round and triangular rooms, flower gardens that creep through the walls and roofs so low that the kids use them as playgrounds.

In translating the two ideas into reality, the bearded young Henken has, at various times, found himself working as a butcher, serving an apprenticeship under Wright, pleading with mortgage companies, tracing lost persons, laboring as a stonemason and persuading an assortment of businessmen and office workers to forsake their cash registers and typewriters in order to do palm-blistering work on their own homes.

Henken says he wouldn't do it again for a million dollars. On the other hand, he wouldn't take a million dollars for his experience in helping build the community, which soon will have assets listed at just about that figure.

The homes are so unusual that a conventional contractor would throw up his hands at sight of the first elevation. If you visited Usonia today you'd probably find Henken on one of the building sites showing the workmen how to pour a concrete bathtub right into the foundation, or build a fireplace that will draw with an almighty roar.

Each home has a personality of its own that seems to wrap itself right around its family. There are some features, though, that are common to virtually all the buildings. The first is a minus factor—you won't find a basement, attic, dormer or guillotine window in Usonia. All the homes are built on a concrete slab, with radiant-heating pipes buried in the floor. The houses are solar-oriented to welcome the warmth of the sun in the winter and lock it out in the summer. (In zero weather, on a sunny day, Henken can work in his shirt sleeves at his drawing board with the door standing wide open less than five feet away.) The houses are designed with as few solid partitions as possible, massive fireplaces, cantilever roofs, broad terraces and sweeping expanses of glass.

Henken's own home is nestled against the side of a hill, partially buried so the winter winds swirl across the roof instead of blowing against the house. So far, the designer has completed one level of an eventual three-unit home. Above the present unit, higher up on the hill, will be his studio,

Inexpensive concrete blocks form a pleasing pattern on one of the Usonia homes designed by Theodore Bower

Jack Holmes photo

Heavy vertical slats permit Mrs. Henken to see the play area, yet they close off kitchen from living area

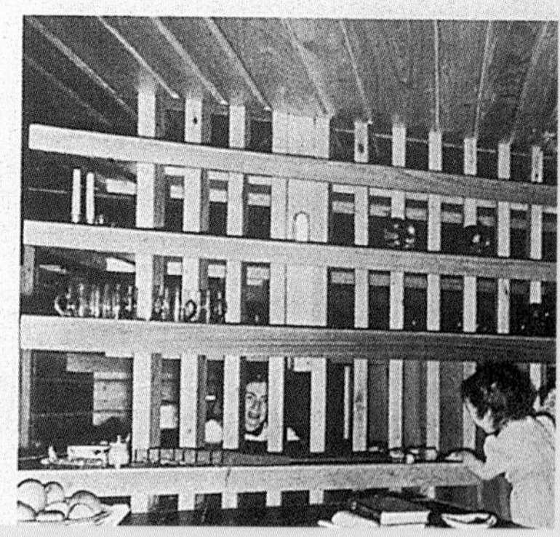

JULY 1951 73

DAVID HENKEN AND USONIA'S HOUSES FEATURED IN THE JULY 1951 EDITION OF *POPULAR MECHANICS*. PICTURED ARE HIS BEN HENKEN (P. 74T), PODELL (P. 73T), AND BRANDON (PP. 74B AND 75T) HOUSES, AND THE SCHEINBAUM HOUSE (P. 72B) BY TED BOWER.

Two full walls of the living room are plate glass. Overhang passes sunlight in winter but not in the summer

Cantilever concrete terrace is ideal for summer living. Tilted roof yields extra light inside the home

connected with the central unit by a covered corridor. Below the present home he'll build a bedroom unit with the roof just the level of today's floor. Henken plans to sod the roof of the bedroom unit; then from the living room, his family can walk straight out onto a broad green terrace. Actually, they'll be standing over the bedroom ceiling.

Inside the present house you can't find a rectangular room anywhere. In fact, you can't seem to find a room at all, for partitions are so subtle they don't appear to be walls. As you walk through the living area, you suddenly find yourself in a little play area for children. Standing there, you are on the edge of the dining area, which apparently melts into the kitchen. Yet from the living room, the kitchen is screened from your view by thick vertical slats, set at an angle like a huge Venetian blind tipped on end. The slats form a strangely efficient wall, for they deny guests the sight of the kitchen, yet they permit Mrs. Henken in the kitchen to hear clearly anything said in the living area and thus to participate in what's going on. She can peer right through the slats, though, at the children's play area a few feet away.

The Henken house is its own furniture and conversely the furniture forms part of the house. Bookcases are partitions, and the back of the sofa is a slanted wall. The attractive sofas in the living area roll out on wheels and convert into spare beds. A long table stretches along the living area, then turns at an abrupt angle around the corner and into the dining space, where it serves as the dining table. But—watch, now—where it turns the corner the two parts are joined by a V-shaped slot. If Mrs. Henken is entertaining quite a number of guests, she merely shoves the dining section of the table out so it joins the other section to form a long straight table which closes off the kitchen. From here she can serve a full meal to guests buffet-style.

The roof is cut into "butterfly" sections, one on top of another, to shed light into the heart of the house. When he designed the kitchen as the core of the building, Henken thought he'd have to install a mechanical ventilating system. As soon as he moved in he discovered that the clerestory windows above the kitchen effectively carry out the heat and cooking odors. As he says—and he's modest about it—"the whole house seems to breath."

Shelves are built into closet doors, the bathtub is poured into the concrete floor slab and a flower garden flows from the terrace outside, through the plate-glass doors, and into the living area. The garden is watered by a perforated tube buried in the soil.

This wasn't at all the house Henken had in mind when he decided to build. At that time, in 1940, he was doodling with a pencil and discussing his ideas with several friends who wanted their own homes, too. Very few had enough money even to walk through the door of a real-estate office. Eventually, the men and their wives formed a cooperative, pooled their piggy-bank savings and started tossing $10 per family into a cooperative kitty each week.

One day quite by accident Henken strolled through the Museum of Modern Art, which was sponsoring a Frank Lloyd Wright exhibit. The show included a model of Wright's "Broadacre City," his still-imaginary Usonia. The young engineer was so impressed that he wrote the famous architect of the cooperative's plans. Would Wright be willing to help? Yes, Wright would be willing to help.

Not long afterward a slightly dazed Henken suddenly discovered that he had given up his job, sold all his belongings and moved with his family to Taliesin, Wright's home at Spring Green, Wis., where he now was an apprentice-architect to Wright. For two

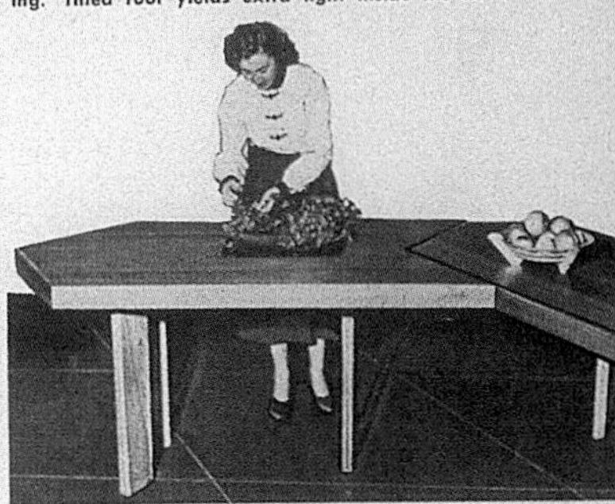

Odd two-part table in Henken's house can be angled either way or set in a straight line as buffet table

Some roofs are so low children can play on them. Tricky foundation lines call for new construction techniques

Henken shows how wall of concrete-block house tilts in at base. Rain drips off, won't penetrate mortar

WHILE MOST APPRENTICES WERE ATTRACTED TO WRIGHT BY THEIR INTEREST IN DESIGN, HENKEN WAS DRAWN BY WRIGHT'S AFFORDABLE USONIAN HOUSES AND HIS CONCEPTS ON COOPERATIVE COMMUNITIES, SUCH AS USONIA 1.

their ideal of an affordable community by demanding costly designs. Henken was caught in the middle.

Usonia left Henken, who bitterly opposed the move to individual ownership and de-emphasis of Wrightian architecture, with a sense of personal loss. Yet, it was more than a loss just for Henken. Usonia marked a highpoint at the end of a chapter in American history: the communitarian cooperative movement. When Usonia ceased to be a true cooperative, a brief but intense era of American optimism died with it.

Henken began his association with Wright as an apprentice at Wright's Taliesin Fellowship in Wisconsin. While most apprentices were attracted to Wright by their interest in design, Henken was drawn by Wright's affordable Usonian houses and his concepts on cooperative communities, such as Usonia 1. That interest clearly resonated with Wright, who had been writing and lecturing on his vision of a better way of life for Usonians (Americans) in "Broadacre" communities. Wright could be severely critical of Henken. For Henken, however, Wright could do no wrong. Henken worshiped him and proclaimed the significance of his work. A number of former apprentices have said that the experience of being at Taliesin with Frank Lloyd Wright had the most profound impact on the rest of their lives.

Henken's missionary-like commitment to Frank Lloyd Wright's ideas and to the cooperative ideal lent a charismatic appeal to his efforts in founding Usonia. The community relied on Henken's relationship with Wright to assure his participation in the design of the community. This was especially important since Usonia's by-laws required Wright's approval of all designs.

Usonia formally contracted with Henken, at first through the building committee, then the architectural association, which became the Design Panel, to implement and supervise the construction of the community. The Design Panel, Henken and Aaron Resnick, was responsible for the design and construction of the community. They developed its roads, water system, and electricity; they marked sites; and they worked with other architects as well as their own clients. They made numerous complicated decisions that were sometimes questioned by members of the cooperative. In addition to enduring a great deal of criticism, their work was made even harder by Usonia's sporadic and restrained cash flow. Henken wrote voluminous notes to himself before and after meetings: comments, suggestions, new agenda items, etc. He wrote communications to the membership as well as anxious pleadings to board members he trusted.

In February 1948 Henken wrote one particularly anguished letter to Jack Masson, the board president. In it he suggested that the board might as well blame him for Usonia's problems since "people are more prone to believe

ANDERSON HOUSE, 1951, BY DAVID HENKEN

top left: THE ANGLED DECK RAILING INCORPORATING A CONTINUOUS BENCH WAS A COMMON FEATURE OF HENKEN'S ABOVE-GRADE DECKS. *© PEDRO E. GUERRERO*

top right: DETAIL OF DECK RAILING

bottom right: SUSAN, PETER, JIM, AND MARGE ANDERSON IN THEIR USONIAN HOME, 1960. *COURTESY THE ANDERSON FAMILY*

top: RALPH MILLER HOUSE, 1949, BY DAVID HENKEN. LIVING ROOM EXTENSION BY AARON RESNICK.
bottom: MASSON HOUSE, 1951, BY DAVID HENKEN.

that, then long-winded explanations." He bitterly described how hard he had worked, "12–15 hours a day for almost one year," and that he had neglected his family completely. The letter, filled with Henken's pain and hurt, described the "shameless misuse and abuse of Aaron [Resnick] and myself.... Aaron and I drew at a little over $1 an hour and paid our draftsmen up to $2.50 and our engineers up to $5. No one would believe it. We have absorbed expenses no other architect would even consider. You will never hear an official complaint." The letter concluded: "I will guarantee you with my honor (which silly enough is most precious to me) the construction of the homes of those people who trust me. For base though I am, I cannot deliberately betray a trust."

Despite his passion, reason, and ability, Henken sometimes found himself alienated from many of his clients and friends. As with most of Usonia's troubles, money was responsible—but not entirely. Most of Henken's work, whether for the community, the Design Panel, or for his own clients, involved new and innovative ideas for which he not infrequently underestimated costs; but he was not alone. He also made some mistakes—designs that functioned poorly or work that had to be redone. Henken, when serving as the architect, expected to be paid the full fee on cost of construction, and, when acting as the builder, all of the mark-ups on construction costs. He rarely acknowledged responsibility for errors or mitigated related charges, and so many of his relationships ended with bitter disputes or litigation. In addition, many Usonians were discontented with the Design Panel's intermediary role with architects and charged that the quality of its services did not warrant the fee amounts.

These issues contributed to Henken's deteriorating relationship with Usonia. When termination of the Design Panel contract was imminent, Henken and Resnick agreed to a reduced fee schedule—ten percent rather than twelve and, under pressure, less in some cases. But fees for unbuilt designs for withdrawn members and for increased costs of construction (changes and additions) remained unresolved. When their partnership ended, Resnick accepted a settlement on these fees, but Henken did not. He had worked long and hard for Usonia with little compensation. He needed and felt entitled to the substantial fees he claimed. Some members, however, felt that he and the panel had served them poorly and should not be paid. (His opponents were inflamed by his visible contempt for the taste, judgment, and integrity of the Domoto clients and other members not committed to seeking Frank Lloyd Wright's approval.) Henken repeatedly sought arbitration of the dispute but the Usonia board of directors, then controlled by his opponents, refused. They reasoned that as an unlicensed architect his claims would not stand up in court. Apparently Henken's lawyers agreed.

The clash between Usonia and Henken had other repercussions. In 1952 Ray and Lillian Kellman joined Usonia, engaged Henken to design their home, and contracted with Henken Builds, Inc. to construct it. Since Henken's dispute with Usonia had not been resolved—he was seeking $20,000 in fees while Usonia was demanding $10,000 of withheld rent—the board feared that Henken Builds would not be able to pay subcontractors and that they would then file liens against Usonia. So the board ruled that Henken could not build in Usonia. Outraged, the Kellmans withdrew and sued Usonia.

Despite these disappointments the years between 1944 and 1955 were a time of tremendous exertion and creativity for David Henken. In that period he founded Usonia Homes, secured the participation of Frank Lloyd Wright, coordinated the selection of land, and designed thirteen houses in Usonia. Among these was a series of houses for himself and his family, including his parents, Benjamin and Frieda Henken; his sister Judeth and her husband Odif Podell; George and Julia Brody (Julia was his sister-in-law); Charlotte and Jerry Podell (Odif's cousin); and later a remodeling of a Tech-Bilt house for his nephew Joshua Podell and wife Roni. He designed for some of the first families, Ralph and Clara Miller and John and Jean Kepler, as well as later members Herb and Ada Brandon, Jack and Ruth Masson, Jim and Margery Anderson, Robert and Bess Milner, Jack and Janet Robertson, and Ken and Janet Silver. He was also hired by

BENJAMIN HENKEN HOUSE, 1951, BY DAVID HENKEN, UNDER CONSTRUCTION. *COSMO-SILEO ASSOCIATES*

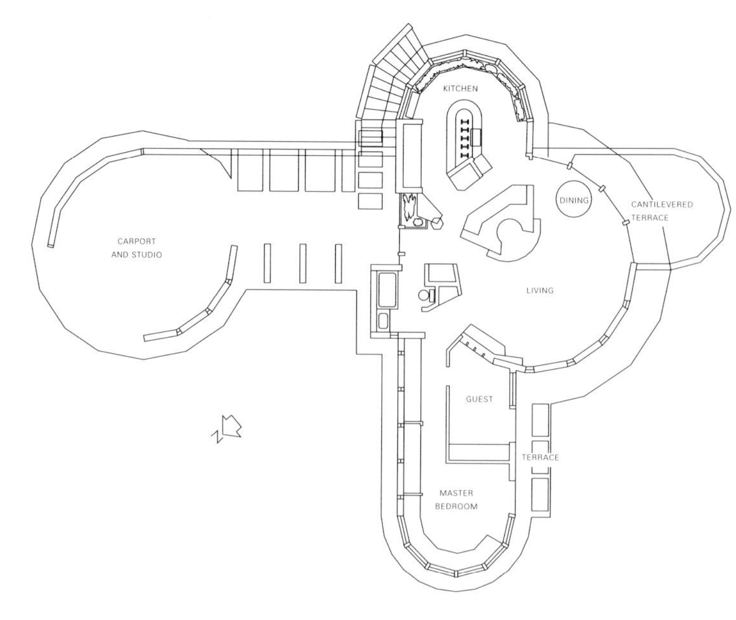

above left: BRODY HOUSE, 1951, BY DAVID HENKEN. INSPIRED BY WRIGHT'S FRIEDMAN HOUSE, HENKEN TRIED HIS HAND AT A CIRCULAR DESIGN.

above right: FLOOR PLAN OF BRODY HOUSE.

REDRAWN BY TOBIAS GUGGENHEIMER STUDIO

left: JOSHUA PODELL HOUSE, 1983. THE IRVING MILLMAN HOUSE, A 1957 TECH-BILT, WAS ACQUIRED BY PODELL AND EXTENSIVELY REMODELED (AS SHOWN HERE) BY HIS UNCLE, DAVID HENKEN. IN 1998, THE HOUSE WAS COMPLETELY REBUILT, RETAINING MUCH OF THE HENKEN DESIGN AND INCORPORATING EXTENSIVE USE OF USONIAN MATERIALS: CYPRESS, STONE, AND RED CONCRETE RADIANT FLOORING (SEE PAGE 170).

Frank Lloyd Wright to help build a full-size model Usonian house as part of an exhibit at the future site of the Guggenheim Museum. Quite a feat for a man who never acquired an architect's license!

But the later years witnessed the steady worsening of his relations with the cooperative. There were huge communication failures among Henken, Resnick, the first five families, and the cooperative. Members were angry because Henken was suing Usonia and because his withheld mortgage payment endangered the survival of the community. By 1953 matters had come to a crisis. Financial disputes, personal grudges, and arguments over the cooperative spirit and Wrightian principles made the meetings of that year among the worst in the community's history. These battles were harsh because they addressed not just Henken, who had attracted such powerful feelings of loyalty and ambivalence, but also the founding principals of Usonia. To some, a vote against Henken was a vote against Usonia. To a majority, however, economic survival seemed at stake.

Neither Henken nor the community would compromise, and in 1955, after the reorganization, the board of directors started legal action to settle the dispute with Henken. His parents, Ben and Frieda, whose home was adjacent to his, also had financial differences with Usonia and joined David in his defense. It concluded with both families separating from membership in Usonia. After that, they owned their individual sites and access road, Wright Way, and paid regular dues for use of Usonia water and roads. But they were no longer Usonia members and so were not charged any other Usonia costs. (Henken lived in his house in Usonia until he died in 1987.)

"WE HAVE COME TO A WILDERNESS, IN THE WOODS, AND HAVE CREATED A WORLD-FAMOUS COMMUNITY. . . . ALL ARE HELD TOGETHER BY WRIGHT'S PERVASIVE INFLUENCE, ALL APPEARING TO GROW OUT OF THE EARTH, BLENDING INTO THE ENHANCED ENVIRONMENT."

Henken continued to design and build, including Frank Lloyd Wright's 1956 addition to the Reisley House, but after several years Henken Builds was forced into bankruptcy. Henken took a job as a design administrator at a college in Maine and after a few years a similar job at a college in New York. His wife Priscilla died in 1969—these were not good times. But Henken's role in Usonia's creation was well known. Architects, scholars, and others sought him out to learn about Usonia and Frank Lloyd Wright's participation.

In 1984 Henken became the principal resource for the Hudson River Museum's exhibition, "Realizations of Usonia, Frank Lloyd Wright in Westchester." He helped the museum acquire photographs, drawings, and models from the Frank Lloyd Wright Foundation and other sources. He worked with Pedro Guerrero, often referred to as "Mr. Wright's photographer," to include his photographs of the community and some of Wright's visits to Usonia. Henken also organized panel discussions with architects, historians, and former apprentices. The exhibition was among the most successful in history of the museum.

For Henken the newfound attention and accolades must have made him feel like the Phoenix arising from the ashes. In the catalog that accompanied the exhibit, Henken wrote an essay, "*Usonia Homes...A Summing Up*," half of which was devoted to the original terms of the cooperative, and half to his reflections on what might have been. With evident pride he described Usonia's successes as well as his view of its failures: "We have come to a wilderness, in the woods, and have created a world-famous community. As a microcosm of society, we have both wonderful neighbors...and the other variety. We have some beautiful buildings and some mediocrities...but all are held together by Wright's pervasive influence, all appearing to grow out of the earth, blending into the enhanced environment."

On June 6, 1984, Henken appeared on the front page of the *New York Times* in an article by architecture critic Paul Goldberger describing a "lost" Frank Lloyd Wright house that had been miraculously found. A photo illustrating the article showed Henken proudly holding a part from the house. The lost house was the full-scale Usonian model that Henken had helped build for Wright on the future site of the Guggenheim Museum. When the house was dismantled in 1954, Wright planned to sell it, but the transaction fell through. Since Henken had helped dismantle the house, Wright asked him to store it and find another buyer. Henken kept the pieces of the house in a shed at his home in Usonia, but after several efforts to find a buyer failed, it was forgotten.

Thirty years later, as the public began to show renewed interest in Wright, Henken decided to donate the house to public television station WNET's fund-raising auction, with the proviso that the buyer engage him to provide the working drawings for its reconstruction. The buyer, Thomas Monaghan, the founder of Domino's Pizza and an avid collector of Frank Lloyd Wright artifacts, paid the station $113,000. In 1987 Henken traveled to Ann Arbor, Michigan, site of Domino's headquarters, to consider sites on which to reconstruct the house. Monaghan sent a car to Henken's hotel to pick him up, but Henken did not make his appointment. In the hotel elevator, on his way down to the first floor, Henken suffered a cerebral hemorrhage and died.

A reporter for a Westchester newspaper wrote a story on Henken's death that diminished his role in building Usonia. It seemed wrong and unfair. Jesse Zel Lurie a Usonian who had been one of Henken's severest opponents and a Domoto client, wrote to correct the story.

> David T. Henken, the founder of Usonia Homes–A Cooperative, Inc., was buried today. David was our Moses. Thirty-five years ago he led us out of the Egypt of New York City to the promised land of Mt. Pleasant. And, like Moses, he was not given the privilege of implementing his dream. Others did so. Others completed a unique cooperative community of forty-eight showcase homes. We, who benefited from David's dream, were able to bring up our families in harmony with our environment and our neighbors. This was David's conception and we and our children shall always be grateful to him. May he rest in peace.

REALIZATIONS
OF
USONIA
FRANK
LLOYD
WRIGHT
IN
WESTCHESTER

above: HENKEN, PHOTOGRAPHER PEDRO GUERRERO, AND ANNE BAXTER (WRIGHT'S GRANDDAUGHTER) AT THE EXHIBITION. THE PHOTO OF WRIGHT ON THE WALL WAS TAKEN IN THE REISLEY HOUSE. *COURTESY PATRICIA HENKEN*

left: COVER OF CATALOG PUBLISHED TO ACCOMPANY A 1984 EXHIBITION ON USONIA AT THE HUDSON RIVER MUSEUM, FOR WHICH HENKEN WAS A PRINCIPAL RESOURCE. *THE HUDSON RIVER MUSEUM OF WESTCHESTER, INC.*

Chapter Eight COMMUNITY LIFE AND ACTIVITIES

AS USONIA TOOK SHAPE IT ATTRACTED HUNDREDS OF CURIOUS VISITORS, ALTHOUGH IT COULD STILL BE HARD TO FIND. TRUDE VICTOR RECALLED THAT "IN THE OLD DAYS, NOBODY COULD FIND US. WE WERE NOTHING BUT SOME DIRT ROADS GOING OFF INTO THE WOODS. IF YOU WERE HAVING PEOPLE OVER FROM OUTSIDE, YOU HAD TO SCHEDULE YOUR PARTIES TWO HOURS EARLIER SO THEY'D BEGIN AT THE USUAL TIME." AMONG THE MOST CURIOUS WERE THOSE WHO LIVED IN NEARBY VILLAGES, SOME OF WHOM WERE DISTURBED BY THE radical architecture, the cooperative liberal philosophy, and other ideals of the newcomers. Pleasantville, a Republican stronghold in prosperous Westchester County, was almost completely white, almost completely middle to upper middle class, and predominantly Christian. Usonians were from New York City, virtually all were Democrats, and many were Jews. Pleasantville was and remains a more diverse community than many in Westchester (it even had a co-op food store, a major attraction for Usonians) and most of Pleasantville's residents were content to live and let live—but some in Pleasantville, Thornwood, and surrounding communities were suspicious. Socially, Usonia was self-sufficient and thus, perhaps, a bit ingrown. To some of the long-established families and working-class townspeople, Usonia seemed strange, elitist, and radical. Political differences (and what some felt were ethnic ones as well) drove subtle wedges between Usonia and its neighbors. One politician referred to Usonians as "those Commie-liberals living in the woods in those kooky houses."

While about two-thirds of the Usonians were Jewish, few, if any, had communist sympathies and none were rich. Eight members—Rick Caro, Gertrude and Arthur Bier, Max and Trude Victor, Isaiah Lew, and Lisette and Jack Hillesum—were Jews who had escaped the horrors of Hitlerian Europe to find a paradise in Usonia. At one time in the emphatically secular community, fourteen families had ties to the newly formed Ethical Society of Northern Westchester, a humanist philosophical movement that is a recognized alternative religion. Most Usonians were professionals of moderate means just beginning their careers. In time a few would indeed become wealthy, and

TOASTING MARSHMALLOWS AT ORCHARD BROOK, SEPTEMBER 1962.

the community would acquire a reputation as an upper-class haven, though Usonians never considered themselves upper class. The thought of Usonia as an enclave for elitist millionaires would have appalled the founders.

Perhaps some suspicion and curiosity arose because of Usonia's physical isolation from the more populated nearby communities. Usonia is in an unincorporated part of the Town of Mount Pleasant. Though approximately equally distant from the villages of Armonk, Thornwood, Chappaqua, and Pleasantville, Usonia is served by the Pleasantville post office. Woods surround the land, which is itself wooded. The Kensico Reservoir borders the property on the south and east. The generations-old Bard's farm and the estate of State Senator Seabury Mastick stood to the west.

USONIA AND TOWN SERVICES

At its founding Usonia was in a geographically large but sparsely populated school district known as Bear Ridge, which included parts of the adjoining Towns of North Castle and New Castle. The district, which dated from the Civil War, once operated in the one-room schoolhouse adjacent to Usonia's land, but had long since contracted to send pupils to the nearby communities. Priscilla Henken found out that Usonia's children could be sent to any of them. The district superintendent was anxious to know how many would be registered the following year, 1948, as ten new children would increase the district's budget by twenty-five percent. Usonia chose Pleasantville, which had good schools and was able to provide transportation. (Henken later became a beloved teacher of English at Pleasantville High School.) Usonia's children composed a chant that they sang on the bus on the way to school:

We're Usonians born,
We're Usonians bred,
And when we die
We're Usonians dead—
Oh it's rah, rah, Usonia, Usonia,
Rah, rah, Usonia, Usonia,
Rah, rah, Usonia,
Rah, rah, rah.

By the 1960s, with much of the vacant land in the Bear Ridge school district being developed with new housing, the number of schoolchildren was many times the forty or so that attended in 1948. The New York State Department of Education recommended that Pleasantville consolidate with Bear Ridge so that its high school would have a large enough student population to offer a diversity of courses. But Pleasantville voted against the consolidation. This disappointed the Bear Ridge families and left many Usonians concerned about continued prejudice toward the community, a view that was perhaps a bit paranoid, as Usonia was not a major part of the district.

After discussions with the neighboring towns, Bear Ridge and Armonk decided to form a new school district, Byram Hills. Usonians felt they had a say in creating the system—as they had in building their homes and community. Sid Miller served on the school board for many years, while Irene (Jupe) Lurie and other Usonians were also active in school matters. Growing awareness of the excellent Byram Hills schools was a source of pride for its community. Real-estate values increased, as did the often-unwelcome development of housing that would gradually occupy much of the nearby open land.

Young Editors Publish Newspaper

EDITORS AT WORK: Ann Scheinbaum, left, and Susan Anderson, celebrated their first anniversary this month as editors of Usonia Chatter, neighborhood newspaper for the Usonia Homes development on Bear Ridge Road Pleasantville. The girls gather news and ads for their monthly publication which sells for five cents a copy or 50 cents yearly subscription. Ads have been selling for one cent a line but are being increased to five cents. The girls do the delivering themselves to 40 regular subscribers. Ann is a fifth grader, and Susan, a sixth grader, at the Bedford Road School.

—Staff photo by Litchfield

No.18 USONIA CHATTER MARCH,1959

Editors-Susan Anderson and Ann Scheinbaum

News

The Siegels got a brown poodle named "Abbie"

The Siegels and Scheiners went to the P.A.A. circus. The Scheiners grandparents went too.

Jojo Resnick learned to ski.

Mr. and Mrs. A.Resnick are going to the theater March 6.

The Parkers went to the P.A.A. circus and so did Bobby and the S.Millers.

Bobby,Sid and Paul went to see "Sunrise at Campobello"

Irene Scheinbaum and Gail Silver had a nursery school on Sunday and it waa a great suocess.The children that were there were:Leslie Resnick,Barbara Reisley, Jimmy Scheiner,Ralph Tamlyn,and Carol Parker. They all had a good time (we hope).

The P.Benzers don't like all the dogs coming to their house.

Karen Benzer has a mechanical rabbit that drinks milk.

Irene and Susan Bier went skiing alone on Washington's Birthday. The skiing was wonderful. Gertrude and Arthur Bier went to Eastover to sk to ski but there waa no snow so they went swimming to get exercise in an indoor pool.

Michael and Matthew Gabel are making puppets building a theater and intend to give a show in the Spring.

Naomi Harris got a bird for her birthday.Ethan Harris got a scholarship. Mr. Harris is making a table for Naomi with a picture of a bird on it made of tile.

Rompy, the Kepler's dog had six puppies.Whoever wants one call the Keplers.

Zel Lurie had an eye infection but he's all right.

Alan Lew was one of the people elected to be a teacher on Student Teacher Day.

Winnie and Harry Miller had their 21 anniversary in March. They are going to Europe April 29.

The Anderson's cats have l st a lot of their hair and the Andersons don't know if both of them should have pills or if the diet they are on will do.

NOTICE - Dalcroze will hold open classes on Thursday,March 19 at the Methodist Church from 12:00 noon to 5:30 P.M....Everybody welcome.

Birthdays

Ann Wax-Feb.24 Jack Wax Feb.5 (sorry we midsed these)

Mr. Glass-March 17

Ethen and Michael Harris-March 20

Meri Henken-March 22 and as an honor of the occasion she will go to the Rivoli.

Tuffy Glass will be nine years old in March.

Ads

Susan Anderson is available for baby sitting.

Kendy Kepler ia available for baby sitting any time of the week.

David Serlin does odd jobs. Call Ro9-2009

Ann Scheinbaum and Susan Anderson are having a school for children kindergarten through first grade. Everyone welcome.Call RO9-1704

Don't miss T om-Two-Arrows- a xxxxx real real Indian.March 14 2:00 and 3:30 P.M. Get tickets from Ellen Berman-50¢

Editorial

Happy Easter and Passover

left: FOR SEVERAL YEARS ANN SCHEINBAUM AND SUSAN ANDERSON GATHERED COMMUNITY NEWS AND PUBLISHED THE MONTHLY *USONIA CHATTER.* *PATENT TRADER*

right: *USONIA CHATTER* FROM MARCH 1959. *COLLECTION ROLAND REISLEY*

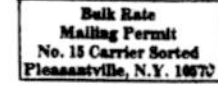

Pleasantville Post

Serving the Town of Mount Pleasant and the Village of Pleasantville

Number 29 — Pleasantville, N.Y., Wednesday, March 9 1983 — 30 Cents A Copy, $12.00 A Year

Usonia gets fire protection from P'ville, after 35 years

by Barbara Dutton Dretzin

After 35 years without official fire protection, Usonia, a 95-acre community of 48 families in the northeast corner of Mt. Pleasant, is to become a new fire protection district within the area served by the Pleasantville Fire Department.

"This is the culmination of about 20 years of work" said Mt. Pleasant Town Supervisor Michael Rovello, at the March 1 Town Board work session, when he announced that the Pleasantville Fire Department had voted on Feb. 22 to provide protection for the proposed new district after "certain conditions are met." Until now, none of the fire departments in the area had been willing to contract to serve the community

The lessening tensions between Usonia and the nearby villages seemed to have relaxed in all aspects but one—Usonia had no fire protection. In 1977, twenty-nine years after the first homes were occupied, a reporter for the *New York Times* wrote: "By most accounts Mr. Wright achieved his 'organic unity', making Usonia a rarity. Unfortunately, the community has become a rarity on another score: it is perhaps the only community in the state that does not have fire protection." One state official told the reporter, "Usonia is unique among inhabited areas—a fire protection no-man's land."

Usonia had sought annexation to the five nearby volunteer fire districts, Thornwood, Pleasantville, Chappaqua, Armonk, and Hawthorne, and was turned down by all. The common reasons stated for the decision were the hazards created by the community's narrow, winding roads that follow the natural rises and folds of the terrain, the lack of an adequate water system, the lack of fire hydrants, and fears that insurance companies would not cover injuries to volunteers and damage to equipment responding to Usonia fire. Usonians however pointed out that areas with similar conditions were included in each of the districts, and they were convinced that coverage was withheld for "other reasons."

Until 1961 Usonia maintained an informal arrangement with the Thornwood fire department and then a similar arrangement with Pleasantville until 1974. Both, however, declined more formal arrangements. Fortunately only a few small house fires and brush fires had occurred in Usonia and help had always come. In April 1976, however, there was a large brush fire and the Pleasantville, Chappaqua, and Thornwood fire departments refused to respond. For several hours housewives in

Usonia and a number of elderly residents battled the fire with shovels and brooms until the Armonk firemen decided to help. The community sought help from town and county executives, from the governor and state attorney general. They responded with sympathetic efforts, but to no avail. Usonians were given no choice but to organize their own fire brigade.

Usonians also had concerns over their water supply. The original well along with a second well was generally adequate, but during a drought period the quantity and quality of the water was reduced. The system was vulnerable to frequent pipe breaks and failures of electricity after storms. The tower held enough water for about one day so when power was off for several days, or until breaks were uncovered and repaired, homes were without water. Change arrived in the early 1980s with the impending development of the unprotected land adjacent to Usonia. There would be 140 homes on land which was also contiguous to the fire district. To exclude Usonia would have been difficult. The town of Mount Pleasant would have to extend its water lines. Usonians were happily shocked when, by means of a bond issue, the town agreed to take over Usonia's water system and supply water from its mains. This was a very significant milestone as it also provided the water needed for fire protection. Finally, in March 1983, the Pleasantville Fire Department voted to extend coverage to Usonia. It took thirty-five years and the prodigious efforts of many Usonians including Bob Siegel, Merrill Sobie, Les Lupert, and Walter Tamlyn who helped with the extended negotiation and litigation, and Jim Anderson and Janet Silver who led in the training of the short-lived fire brigade, which fortunately did not have to fight any fires.

COMMUNITY BUILDING

As Usonians built their houses they also began to make improvements on the community land. Early Usonians shared hardship, idealism, and anxiety. For years, the roads, covered in crushed rock, went unpaved, prompting Odif Podell's remark, "We survived wheeling baby carriages uphill on rocky paths." Wright's planned community house and farm unit were never built, but the land he allotted for recreation, the South Field, was soon used for a baseball field, a play area for smaller children, and a communal picnic and campfire area. The July 4th father–son baseball game became a ritual enjoyed by all. One of the first community projects was creating Orchard Brook Pool, the Swimming Hole, by damming a small stream (a headwater of the Bronx River) in a northeast corner of Usonia. Because Usonia would not require members to pay for "luxuries," the Orchard Brook Pool Club subcooperative was formed in 1950. In another year water began filling the pond. To create a "beach" members spread a truckload of sand along the sunny shore (a ritual to be repeated every few years as the sand washed away). Soon, fathers, working with carpenters, built a float for diving.

Picturesque in a rough-and-ready way at the foot of a huge weeping willow tree, the Swimming Hole quickly became yet another bonding site, a place where parents and children could spend long summer hours. It featured roped sections arranged by depth (and age of swimmer): a shallow end for the babies, a middle end for seven- and eight-year-olds, which featured some big rocks for sunning; and a deep end, where older kids and adults swam. These former city families could lounge around a real country swimming hole, one they had created

THESE FORMER CITY FAMILIES COULD LOUNGE AROUND A REAL COUNTRY SWIMMING HOLE, ONE THEY HAD CREATED THEMSELVES, WATCH THEIR CHILDREN PLAY AND LEARN TO SWIM, AND REFLECT THAT THEY HAD FINALLY ACHIEVED WHAT THEY HAD COME FOR.

themselves, toss horseshoes, play bridge, gossip, and watch their children play, make friends, and learn to swim, and reflect (when they were not worrying about house payments) that they had finally achieved what they had come for. That is why the Swimming Hole has taken on an almost mythical place in the memories of the original Usonians and their children.

By the early 1970s, as most Usonian children were finishing high school or college, use of the Orchard Brook Pool declined and maintaining the facility presented problems; the dam needed to be completely rebuilt. The pool, an earth-lined pond, was not crystal clear, and though beloved, was also called "Mud Hole" and "Coffee Lake." "If you went in with a white bathing suit, you came out mud colored," recalled Amy Resnick. Much as its naturalistic presence appealed to many because "it fit—it was more like Usonia," other members longed for a clean, tiled pool with filtered, clear water, but cost was an obstacle. By 1980 interest in a new pool grew enough to make it feasible. Aaron Resnick designed a scheme that was popular and affordable and that would be built at the South Field, where, in 1958, a sub-co-op, the South Field Tennis Club, built two courts. Members who had never played tennis learned how. In July 1981 the South Field Pool opened with a joyous celebration and a reunion of all Usonian generations. A huge cake bore the legend "Southfield Pool, Hooray!" Its lawns and picnic area again provided Usonians a place to socialize and hold holiday events.

COMMUNITY ACTION

As the fathers had developed the pool, so the mothers were mainly responsible for organizing the playgroup. Beginning in 1950 a nursery and playgroup for toddlers operated during the summer. "We did it like we did everything," Bobbie Miller recalled. "Someone said they wanted a playgroup, and we got together and formed one." At first it was the mothers themselves who did all the work. Summer mornings began with an assemblage of kids and moms starting the day with a walk through the woods to the Swimming Hole to paddle in the shallow end. James and Ginny Parker remembered how the playgroup was "especially attractive to a couple planning to have children." It was one of the reasons that compelled them to move to Usonia.

For some two-career families, a nursery was a necessity; for others, it was a good way for adults to share time together; for all involved, it was an intensely unifying experience. The summer playgroup was a "joyous experience for our kids," said Odif Podell. Mothers organized special projects for their groups, including nature walks, treasure hunts, plays, and tree-house building. Fathers knocked together a little storage shed for the group. There were circus shows, pajama parties, arts and crafts projects, and the oft-remembered greased watermelon races.

clockwise from top left: ORCHARD BROOK POOL, GROUP ON SAND "BEACH," 1963; PICNIC AT SOUTH FIELD POOL, 1989; GROUP SHOT OF TENNIS REGULARS OF THE SOUTH FIELD TENNIS CLUB, 1988 *ODIF PODELL*; PLAYGROUP AT TREEHOUSE, 1964.

Eventually, outside teachers and counselors were hired, and children from outside the neighborhood participated. Usonia's playgroup became a true summer camp. It even caught the attention of Dorothy Barclay, the education editor of the *New York Times*, who wrote, "Parents themselves, brought together actively in a project all believe in, get to know one another far better than they would over the teacups or bridge table." As the median age of Usonian children grew, the playgroup declined and was eventually discontinued—although, in what is probably a permanent practice, Usonian families still baby-sit for one another.

It seemed that whenever there was a need or a special interest, individual Usonians rose to the occasion with semiformal groups and services of their own. Jack Wax established a community garden. Jupe Lurie and Ottilie Auerbach taught the girls to cook. Lucille Scheinbaum ran an exercise class for adults and dance classes for children. Istar Glass, a professional dancer, also gave informal dance lessons. A madrigals singing group that met at the Friedman House blossomed into the Pleasantville Cantata Singers. There was also a Usonian children's orchestra.

Even some medical issues were handled within the community. Dr. Arthur Bier and dentists Sidney Benzer and Isaiah Lew were among Usonia's early members. They practiced in New York City and before long also opened local offices nearby. Within Usonia they gladly provided emergency attention when needed. Kids remember Dr. Bier appearing at the Quonset hut to check them for ringworm or the occasional cuts and bruises. But he also provided heroic service. In the mid-1950s, before the Salk vaccine became available, Walter and Jean Tamlyn and their son Robert were hospitalized with polio, and the community panicked. As a heavy snowstorm had blocked the roads, Dr. Bier trudged through the snow to administer gamma globulin shots to Usonians.

A PLAQUE IN KAMALAPUR

In accordance with its by-laws, Usonia may not support any political or religious activity. Individuals, of course, may do as they wish. In solidly Republican northern Westchester County it was not surprising that a group of Usonians found their way to the local Democratic organization. Odif Podell once ran for local office, as did Sam Resnick. Individually and in groups, Usonians have also been social-political activists in many local, national, and international causes, ranging from school politics, civil rights, sane nuclear policy, and national elections.

In the late 1950s Jack Robertson, a Usonian and professor of education at New York University, spent a year in Asia on a UNESCO project studying underprivileged countries. He wrote back to Usonians describing his observations of poverty there. Members discussed his letter at a Usonia cocktail party. "Yesterday, when it was my turn to drive the ballet lesson car pool," one woman said, "I was listening to those kids. They were making fun of a classmate who wore the same dress three days in a row. They haven't the foggiest notion how the rest of the world lives." Others agreed, "How can poverty seem real to our children when we don't act as if it's our responsibility?"

Twenty-three Usonian families, chaired by Jack Robertson, banded together to form People to People, Inc. (PTP). It purposed: "We want to give tools to help others help themselves. . . . We want our children and our families to know people in other sections of the world. . . . The gap between the rich and the poor is as great a threat to peace as the arms race." This was truly a statement for its time, with echoes of the vision of the Peace Corps. PTP sought both to help the less fortunate and to teach its children what they could not know, growing up in the demi-paradise their parents and architects had created for them.

Robertson invited several Indian graduate students to meet the Usonians and discuss possible means of assistance. One of the students, C. R. Seshu, had recently arrived in the United States from the small village of Kamalapur, a farming community of about one-hundred families. They had transportation problems, no modern farming equipment, and no school. Five or six families were educated, otherwise literacy was about one percent.

By chance Usonians Jane and Martin Scheiner had scheduled a trip to India to inspect medical equipment made by their company, and they agreed to visit the village. After a long journey the Scheiners found Kamalapur, a clean, destitute village whose people followed them around "like a troop of emaciated scarecrows." At the excited village meeting they asked how Usonia could help, and a consensus arose that Kamalapur needed a school more than anything else. Four thousand rupees (about eight hundred dollars) would build a school, and another six hundred dollars would pay a teacher for two years, after which the government might pick up the salary. Seshu and the Usonians agreed that a school would be of permanent value.

The Scheiners returned, showed their photographs, and PTP collected enough to build the school and pay the teacher. The villagers themselves shaped and baked the adobe bricks, and did much of the construction. A plaque on the school reads, "This school was built by citizens of Pleasantville, New York, U.S.A., and Kamalapur, India, as an expression of mutual understanding." Usonian Jane Scheiner described the project in an article for *Progressive* magazine.

CELEBRATIONS

A wonderful Usonian tradition, that of holding communal gatherings on major holidays, began with a New Year's Eve party in 1949. Concerns over late-night driving, drinking, baby sitting arrangements, and expense easily convinced Usonians to organize their own party. Celebrations on the Fourth of July and Labor Day followed. Members bonded as they anticipated and organized one occasion after another, year after year. Fay and Rowland Watts recalled: "We started off having an annual New Year's Eve party at someone's house, with the whole community joining in to decorate and provide food and entertainment. Other happy events were celebrated: births, confirmations, weddings. As time went on we also celebrated a life even as it came to an end."

"We were very aware of cooperative aspects," added Lucille Scheinbaum. "For instance, once a month we had a birthday party for children who had birthdays during that month. There was a fund to buy presents for those children. That is almost a metaphor for the way we thought. Everything was community. In the beginning no one ever had a party without inviting everyone."

These events featured food, picnics or pot-lucks, conversation, and—depending on the season—swimming races, games, dancing, and at times vociferous discussions of politics and architecture. For over fifty years Usonians have enjoyed being together at these events.

Usonia's most important celebration was its fiftieth anniversary, celebrated on July 31, 1994. Two-hundred-and-fifty people—former members, children, grandchildren,

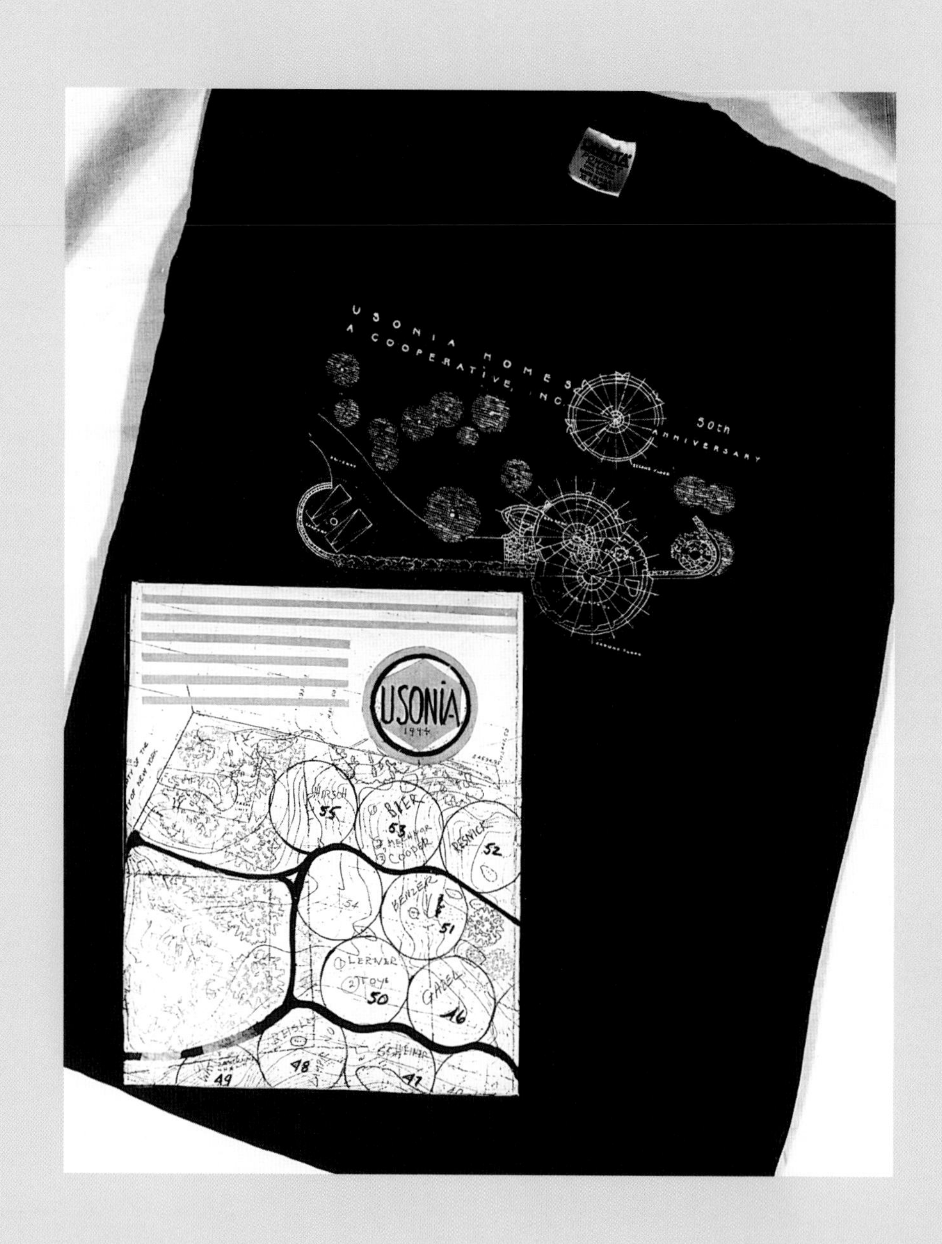
USONIA HOMES
A COOPERATIVE, INC.
50th
ANNIVERSARY
USONIA
1944

builders, and architects, some coming from great distances—gathered to renew friendships and celebrate what together they had experienced and accomplished.

They had all been encouraged to send personal reminiscences and photographs recalling Usonia's creation. Some brought photos, others brought home movies. One film showed Frank Lloyd Wright in stately progress, walking around the building site on a winter's day in 1948. As the film flickered across the screen, elderly Usonians and builders watched images of their younger selves wheelbarrowing dirt and rock, hammering nails, scrambling up hills of lumber, helping to wrest houses into being. As they watched, there was a sense, not only of a great stretch of time having passed, but also of something tremendous and difficult having been achieved. Survival was the watchword for this reunion—not just of people, but of ideals.

In all, one-hundred-and-twenty pages of personal recollections were submitted for the reunion. Duplicated and bound with a cover featuring Wright's historic site plan, they were distributed to all. One thing seemed clear in paging through this book of memories: Usonia was obviously a wonderful place for a child to grow up. As Amy Resnick put it, the children "knew the location of the refrigerator in virtually every home and could identify the bark of each of the forty dogs," in Usonia. Carol Lamm fondly recalled "the sleep-overs where you could pedal your bike home in the morning still wearing your baby-doll pajamas."

One of the most expressive and detailed childhood memories came from Betsy Glass: "Usonia raised me, taught me powerfully. It is not a thing I did or have or a place I live.... Usonia is a spirit, an eternal state of being. It is who I was, am, and always will be. I thank the passionate pioneer women and men of Usonia... my mentors, teachers, role-models, 'aunts, uncles and cousins,' now friends and family... for shaping who I am: a possibility for art, communication, education, collaboration, and a strong link in this infinite chain of dreams."

Betsy's eloquent reminiscence is not unlike those of other next generation Usonians, such as Carol Lamm: "There are no words that could adequately convey what growing up in Usonia meant to me," she wrote. "For better or worse Usonia helped mold and shape me in mind, body, and spirit. Looking back, there are thousands of disjointed memories that run on together.... I'm one of the lucky ones. I got to have a whole other set of memories as a Usonian parent as well. I am so grateful that my children were able to experience a Usonia of their own—different to be sure—but still a unique and love-filled experience that will stay with them always as it has with me."

Photographs of children cram many Usonian albums and were very much in evidence at the reunion: crowds of children playing, biking swimming together. Togetherness among equals marked the children's world—and so did freedom. As Gail Silver wrote: "There were no walls restricting us as we played hide and seek around the wood, glass and stone houses, which blended so perfectly with nature. All of Usonia was ours; the only walls and fences were those that marked the outer boundaries of Usonia, and those only added to our adventures." Another Usonian remarked, "The children... think they are better people for having been brought up here. And we think so, too."

Frank Lloyd Wright would have appreciated that passage. Families living a life "blended so perfectly with nature" was what he had profoundly preached. Usonians had made good on his vision and were enjoying it.

opposite: FIFTIETH-ANNIVERSARY T-SHIRT AND SOUVENIR BOOK.
overleaf: GROUP PHOTOGRAPH OF FIFTIETH ANNIVERSARY.

Chapter Nine USONIA REVISITED

USONIA'S APPARENT SUCCESS AS A COMMUNITY—ITS LONGEVITY, STABILITY, AND THE ONGOING ENTHUSIASM OF ITS MEMBERS—HAS CHALLENGED SCHOLARS, VISITORS, AND EVEN ITS OWN MEMBERS TO EXPLAIN IT. CLEARLY THE VISION OF THE FOUNDERS AND FRANK LLOYD WRIGHT WERE SIGNIFICANT, BUT IT WAS THE PEOPLE WHO RESPONDED TO THEIR IDEAS AND WORKED TOGETHER TO IMPLEMENT THEM THAT MADE USONIA HAPPEN. THESE WERE NOT EXTRAORDINARY PEOPLE, BUT SOMEHOW THEIR SHARED NEEDS AND interests, their commitment, courage, social idealism, and vision were the perfect ingredients to make Usonia last.

When I set out to document this history and to interview Usonia's members, I explained: "I'm trying to find out who were we that came to this adventure? What actually happened? And how have we experienced it?" More or less the same questions interested Usonian Johanna Cooper in 1983, writer John Timpane in 1994, and, over the years, many students, for grade-school papers to graduate theses.

"What happened" has been described in previous chapters. Yet, important and interrelated questions remain: What difference did living in artistic homes make for their lives—and more generally, what difference did living in Usonia make? What made Usonia last? What were the factors that brought these families through crisis after crisis to forge this community? Most Usonians reacted in exactly the same way to these questions. It was the surrounding land, their houses, the ambience of natural, human, and artistic relations reflecting the values in which they had raised families and developed careers that made the difference. "It wouldn't have been the same somewhere else" was a frequent comment.

Judging from the trajectory of their children's lives, the devotion of Usonians to art and to social causes has made a tremendous difference. A part of being Usonian was being artistic. Gertrude Gabel was an art teacher. Sol and Bert Friedman spearheaded music groups. Bette Zais, Amy Resnick, Jim and Marge Anderson, my wife and myself, and others were longtime members of the Cantata Singers. Florence Benzer made fine jewelry. Ada Brandon was a weaver. Mel Smilow, a

THE HILLESUM FAMILY POSE OUTSIDE THEIR NEW USONIAN HOUSE.

COURTESY HILLESUM FAMILY

furniture designer, is also an artist. Jane Scheiner was a freelance writer. Istar Glass was a dancer and actress. She also was a talented interior designer, and contributed her skills to various Usonian houses. Millie Resnick was a painter, a graphic designer, and a professor of art at the College of New Rochelle. She was responsible for aspects of the interiors of several Usonian houses, including her own and some items in the Reisley House. Aaron Resnick was not only an architect but also a poet and pianist. Arnie Zais was a sculptor as well as a business executive, and his house and garden are a gallery of his work. Johanna Cooper designs book jackets and worked at the Museum of African Art.

A few Usonians had to retire before they could explore their interest in the arts. Bob Siegel went to night school to earn an architecture degree after a career in law and business. At 75 Max Victor approached Millie Resnick for art lessons, and he became an accomplished painter; Trude Victor and several other Usonians have his canvasses on their walls.

USONIA'S CHILDREN

Usonia's children share their parents' devotion. Hannah Victor designs jewelry. Jackie Masson is a professional ceramist. Michael Benzer manufactures artistic glass. Annie Scheiner makes artistic flags and banners. Betsy Glass is a dancer and a teacher of folkdance. David Friedman is an accomplished musician. Jessie and Lucy Resnick both practice weaving and graphic design. Pam and Judy Smilow are artists and designers. Architecture, understandably enough, has also attracted some of the children: Judie Benzer, Roger Hirsch, Peter Silson, Eric Lerner, and Gordon Kahn.

Many of the Usonian children have voiced their commitment to social ideals and have linked it to their upbringing in Usonia. That may account for their strong professional interest in social work, law, and the human services. (Six of their mothers became social service professionals, as social workers, psychologists, and therapists.) Debbie Caro is an anthropologist, her brother Alan a social worker. Joanne Siegel became a social worker, Alan Lew a rabbi. Many Usonian children went into law, often for social-activist reasons. Ken Miller, Matt Gabel, and Bruce Parker became lawyers. Bob Brandon and David Watts did public interest law. Linda Watts became a social worker. Steve Wax became a public defender and assistant D.A.; his sister Barbara is a teacher. Doug Berman went into law—"partly," as he put it, "for social reasons, to see if I could do anything to make the world better"—and for a time was treasurer of the State of New Jersey. As an assistant district attorney for the Bronx, Johanna Resnick founded the Domestic Violence Unit.

Children living in Usonia in beautiful houses grew up in freedom: "Artistically, the house gave me the frame to live as I wanted to live, and to bring up my children in the way in which I wanted them to be brought up," said Trude Victor. "My children both chose ways of living I approve of—ways that have a great deal of art and goodness in them. They are still interested in the life of the mind."

Young, passionate, and idealist, Usonians were bent on creating a world in which to have families, and they used this world of art, commitment, and self-reliance as a matrix in which to raise those families with originality and love. Pride emanates from all of them, that they were able to "do all of this," but most of all that they were able to raise their children as they wished. The organic houses, the organic sensibility enriched the humane, open, tolerant culture in which their children grew. Surely an indication of the difference it made to the children is their own recurring tribute to Usonia. Six came back to set up their own homes here (not necessarily in the homes of their parents), while many more keep paying visits. Moving into Usonia is no easy thing. The houses are expensive and come on the market seldom.

Two of Odif and Judy Podell's children returned. Their son Joshua and his wife Roni live in Usonia in a house they acquired over twenty years ago. Another Podell son, Ethan, also lived in Usonia. Lisa Podell Greenberg, the daughter of Jerry and Charlotte Podell, acquired their home in Usonia. Later, needing a larger house, she moved to a nearby community. "There's something about Usonia that will always be with me," she said. "People just don't do things like this any more—but they could. Why not? People have more money now than they did then. Why not?"

Another Usonia child who moved back is Betsy Glass, who lives in her parents' house. She is a passionate upholder of Usonian tradition, and loves the fact that some of the children have come back to settle there. Carol Lamm, daughter of Charlotte and Icy Lew, moved back to Usonia with her husband Bob. The Lamms were able to raise children in Usonia before Bob Lamm's work made it necessary for them to move, reluctantly, elsewhere. Leslie Resnick, daughter of Amy and Sam, and her husband moved back. And Robert and Bess Milner's daughter, Hope, and her husband Merril Sobie raised their children there and have become mainstays in the community. "I almost experience my being as interchangeable with Usonia's," Hope Sobie explained. Five other Usonian children live in homes that are but minutes away.

THE TOUGH QUESTION

The other question I posed to my neighbors was, "How did living in your house in Usonia affect your life?" I wondered, can people know how living next to expressive art in the midst of nature changed their lives? Of course the question elicits replies but the answer, if there is one, may have to be inferred by others.

Aaron Resnick believed that the physical layout of Usonia had much to do with the way the earliest settlers hung together: "We happened to be just the right size. . . . We could plan private lives and still have personal interactions with almost everybody else in the community. We were all involved somehow." Bobbie Miller agreed: "One of the great things is the way the houses are all sited. They're just not along the street, with a great big lawn up to a great big house. They're higgledy-piggledy, hither and yon, with a lot of wildness in between. I think that's great."

Wildness with civilization, privacy with community—Usonians have experienced the kind of balance that Americans have been seeking for two and a half centuries. "Wright's road and site plan was a masterstroke," explained Esther (Harris) Schimmel. "It gave us space and privacy surrounded by nature. The stone and glass that Kan (Kaneji Domoto) integrated with our land has been immensely satisfying." Trude Victor wrote that in her house, designed by Aaron Resnick, "to bring the outside inside, the flow of movement inside to outside, kitchen to dining room, dining to living room, seemed natural and kind of exhilarating."

Sid Miller agreed: "I think the elements of this house and the other Usonian houses that truly make a difference are the elements that bring you so close to nature: all the glass, so you're constantly in touch with birds, and

> WRIGHT WAS AT WAR WITH THE BOX, THE ENCLOSURE OF MOST HOUSES. HE WAS LOOKING FOR A NEW WAY TO DRAMATIZE SPACE. USONIANS GENERALLY BELIEVE THAT LIVING IN SUCH SPACES DID BRING DRAMA AND MEANING TO THEIR DAILY LIVES.

with deer, and with everything else that's around us, the flora and the fauna, things that have been important to us over the many years that we've been here. . . . People, when they come to visit us, even people who know nothing about architecture, realize there's something different going on."

Millie Resnick was adamantly devoted to Usonia: "I wouldn't be able to live anywhere else—unless I have the outdoors. They'll have to carry me out of this place. [Millie died in March 2000.] This house was the haven from the activity that kept us going all day long. . . . The other aspect is that every day, even now, I discover new things. Visually, new things. It's given me a sense of repose, of being one with something out there, which I'd always wanted. It's given me that feeling of belonging to what's out there, of not being separated."

Until the early 1990s—when age increasingly was taking its toll—nearly all Usonians had lived there for a long time and in virtually all of their reminiscences try to describe the profound effect of their Usonian environment. My own remark, often shared with interested visitors—especially architects—is this: "I have lived for over fifty years of my life in this house, and some of those days were pretty terrible days. I've lost two children. I've had triumphs and failures. But, after perhaps 20 years, I came to realize that not one of those days has passed without my seeing, here or there, something beautiful." To which I sometimes add, "Go thou and do likewise."

Much of this is a tribute to Frank Lloyd Wright. All his life, Wright was at war with the box, the rectangular enclosure of most houses. He was always looking for a new way to dramatize space, literally to help people re-experience the corners, rooms, and hallways in which we spend out lives. He was trying to get us to be aware of our lives as we live them, to wake us up, not let us get used to anything, not let life become a habit. Usonians generally believe that living in such spaces did bring drama and meaning to their daily lives. They definitely agree that their houses constantly reveal new and unexpected things.

USONIA'S DESIGNS

Wandering through Usonia one sees houses integrated in the land, looking as though they "belonged there." The Wright houses are unmistakable and the others, while they may lack the overall grammar that Wright attributed to his designs, clearly echo his Usonian vocabulary in their use of glass, masonry, horizontal cypress, clerestory windows, and other features. These houses, carefully placed on their wooded sites, continue to look modern but no longer startle as they did fifty years earlier, perhaps because many of their components have been widely copied.

Twenty-six of Usonia's homes—more than half—were designed by David Henken and Aaron Resnick, thirteen each. They, along with architects Kaneji Domoto, Ted

Bower, Paul Schweikher, and Charles Warner, were greatly influenced by Frank Lloyd Wright and tried to design homes that he would approve. Henken often used angular grids and other innovative devices to produce some dramatic but occasionally awkward spaces. Resnick, on the other hand, was more restrained; he stayed with the right angle and close to budget. His Usonian clients resented the fact that Wright and Henken overshadowed him in the flood of publicity that Usonia received. Resnick had done much of the engineering work on the roads and water system; his houses worked well and he designed several additions to other homes in Usonia. But it was always Wright's organic philosophy of design that set the tone: "In organic architecture the ground itself predetermines all features; the climate modifies them; available means limit them; function shapes them."

While assessing Wright's contribution, it is interesting to note that a few Usonians, although truly appreciative of their organic homes, do not think that Wright's Usonian philosophy is a factor in the success and longevity of the community. Rather, they say, it was the bonds formed in the collective struggle to build Usonia. "They could have been Cape Cod houses," one Usonian said.

Usonia Homes was not the only post-World War II planned cooperative community, but it may be the most successful. Some others include Twenty One Acres in Ardsley, New York, Skyview Acres in Rockland County, New York, and the Wright-designed Parkwyn Village and Galesburg Country Homes, both in Michigan. Despite similar aspirations, Galesburg—which is quite beautiful—never developed beyond five homes and Parkwyn, with four Wright houses, evolved somewhat conventionally and only for a time maintained an active community life. Twenty One Acres built fourteen modern homes in 1950 and functioned as a close community for about twelve years. Skyview Acres, a much larger development, was led by philosophically committed cooperative leaders who were primarily concerned with building lower-cost homes. None of these co-ops lasted the way Usonia has.

A favorite topic among Usonians is why their community endured and others did not. "Fundamentally, it was idealism," said Trude Victor. "[The founders] believed in what they were doing." Esther Schimmel said, "They were mavericks.... They weren't neutral; they were intense." After a laugh, she added, "It was fun living with them."

Fun helps, and so do trials and tribulations. Money problems were a common spur of support and sympathy. Some say that isolation by the outside community also made the group stronger. So did the unrelenting hard work, which Usonians have always accepted as part of the price of being a cooperative.

Some were following the promise of an architecture and the morality it represented. Others were cooperative enthusiasts. All accepted both, but some Usonians were neither architecture buffs nor cooperativists. They simply liked the idea of the community and liked the Usonians they met. Johanna Cooper, who interviewed many of the original Usonians, felt it was a combination of things: "The individuals who made it work, the human bonds between members, the cooperative aspects, the architecture, and the unique match of people who were well-suited to each other and cared about each other.... I believe it was the drive and motivation of the founders. Those were highly motivated people willing to gamble with their lives."

Yet, so much of what they have loved about the quality of their lives in Usonia—the serenity, the balance between an intensely knit community and an intensely fulfilling private life, the contact with the outside world, the refuge from the city, the self-sufficiency—so much is exactly what Wright was preaching in his manifestos about Broadacre City. Wright, of course, did not work the roads or caulk the windows or suffer through the knock-down, drag-out meetings—Usonians themselves did, and, as Wright advocated, they participated in the building of their homes. And they know they have achieved something truly original. But behind much of the physical and social arrangements of Usonia lie ideas in which Wright had a significant part. The organic architecture, the cooperative ownership, the acre sites, winding roads and open land—these are the hallmarks of Wright's Broadacre City. It seems possible that Wright was right.

USONIA TODAY AND TOMORROW

At this writing, fifty-six years after its founding, Usonia has fairly well maintained its unique character. The many architects, scholars, planners, and students who visit Usonia continue to appreciate what they see and learn about the community. Indeed, the National Trust of Historic Preservation and the New York State and Westchester County preservation offices have urged Usonia to seek designation as a National Register Historic District.

But preserving and extending its benefits is a challenge to newer residents in circumstances quite different from those of the founders. Twenty of the original Usonian families, now quite old, and four of their offspring remain in the community. One must wonder if current and future Usonians will find shared values and ideals to enhance their experience of community. If not, how will Usonia evolve?

Virtually all of the thirty or so "newer" Usonians seeking a "nice home in a nice place" were attracted by the homes and the land they saw and what they heard about the community life. But the sense of "connected, extended family" did not necessarily materialize for them. Absent the shared challenges of creating Usonia—and the frequent meetings concerning them—new members are denied the experiences that bonded the original group. As the proportion of longtime members inexorably declines, however, so does Usonia's communitarian quality of life. Many lament it, some hope to revive it, most sadly acknowledge: "That was then, this is now. Things are different."

But the homes and land are not different. The unique physical character of Usonia continues to be admired and enjoyed. Environmental concerns for clean air and water, oceans and forests, but also the *built* environment are quietly shared by most Usonians. Perhaps if Usonians become more conscious of their beneficial connection to the profound, transcendental environmental values asserted by Ralph Waldo Emerson, Henry David Thoreau, Walt Whitman, and Frank Lloyd Wright, they will be invigorated to support actively preservation and protection of their community. Worthwhile buildings and neighborhoods succumb to age, neglect, and improper maintenance as well as aggressive development and sprawl. Active response by Usonians would echo the social and esthetic idealism that enriched the community in earlier years and stimulate pride in knowledgeably preserving Usonia itself.

AERIAL VIEWS OF USONIA AND ITS SURROUNDING LAND SHOW THE CHANGE FROM FARMLAND TO ENCROACHING DEVELOPMENT. THOUGH THIS IS FELT, FROM WITHIN USONIA IT IS HARDLY VISIBLE. ***clockwise from top left:*** 1947 AND 1963. *WESTCHESTER COUNTY DEPARTMENT OF PLANNING;* 2000. *ROBINSON AERIAL SURVEYS*

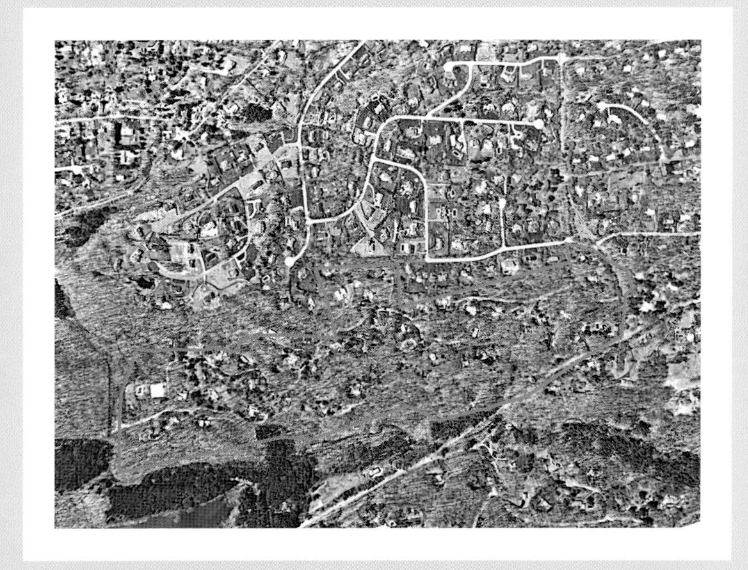

Epilog FRANK LLOYD WRIGHT AND THE REISLEY HOUSE

BUILDING A HOME, A *FIRST* HOME, WITH FRANK LLOYD WRIGHT WAS AN UNEXPECTED, ESPECIALLY EXCITING EXPERIENCE FOR MY WIFE AND ME. THE HOME WRIGHT BROUGHT US, IN THE COMMUNITY HE INSPIRED, HAS ENRICHED OUR LIVES IN WAYS FAR BEYOND WHAT WE COULD ENVISION. THIS IS TRUE NOT ONLY IN OUR IMMEDIATE ENVIRONMENT, BUT ALSO THROUGH THE ENSUING AQUAINTANCE AND FRIENDSHIP WITH INTERESTED ARCHITECTS, STUDENTS, AND HISTORIANS FROM ALL OVER THE WORLD. HENCE THIS ACCOUNT.

Ronny and I married in 1950. I was a physicist, she a psychologist. We lived in a small apartment in New York City. We were interested though not particularly sophisticated in design, but we had some do-it-yourself skills. I had designed some furnishings for the apartment; I had some things made professionally and built some myself. Ronny sewed slipcovers, draperies, and the like.

We were both only children and looked forward to establishing our own home and family. On weekends we drove around the suburbs looking at houses, but couldn't find anything we liked or could afford. David Henken's sister, Judeth Podell, worked in my father's office and told him of "a cooperative community in Westchester building affordable homes, supervised by Frank Lloyd Wright." He told us about it, and we decided to have a look. We liked the people, the place, and the concept and promptly applied to join. We used a wedding present of $2500 intended for a European tour for our membership and site.

AN INTRODUCTION TO WRIGHT

We thought Frank Lloyd Wright was surely out of reach for our architect and were learning about others when Henken suggested that if Wright liked our site and liked us, he might want to design our house. Henken told Wright about us and showed him our land, and reported that Wright expressed interest. Soon afterward I spoke with Wright on the phone—we were hooked.

On October 26, 1950, we sent THE LETTER—our five-page attempt to define ourselves, our $20,000 budget, our needs, interests, the lifestyle we anticipated, the things we thought a great architect should know to design the "perfectly fitted home."

FRANK LLOYD WRIGHT DRAWS A FIREPLACE GRATE FOR THE REISLEY HOME AS ROLAND AND RONNY LOOK ON. *© PEDRO E. GUERRERO*

> Dear Mr. Wright,
>
> I was delighted to learn during our telephone conversation last Friday that you are interested in designing a house for the site my wife and I selected in Usonia. We think it is a beautiful and challenging site. For as long as we have had any architectural awareness, we have profoundly admired your work and your viewpoint. Quite honestly, we are tremendously grateful that, through Usonia, we can now contemplate the lifelong pleasure of living in a house of your design. . . .
>
> We both enjoy books, people, theatre, children, art, music, food, wine, pets, stone, wood, sunlight, grass, glass, sky and trees.
>
> We would like a house to provide us with the feeling of space, light, warmth and integration with the outdoors. We do not like compact, massive structures but prefer a sense of lightness and mobility. We admire your use of large glass areas, cantilevers and the artistic and ingenious use of overhangs. . . . We will not presume to discuss style any further. I am sure that, after we have met, you will make your own analysis of what best suits us. . . .
>
> Once again, Mr. Wright, we are most sincerely grateful for your interest and look forward with excitement to our association.
>
> Sincerely,
>
> Roland Reisley

Wright wrote back to us and invited us to visit Taliesin for a weekend. We did, in November—driving 1400 miles each way. Arriving at Taliesin was unforgettable. We first glimpsed the great graceful building so comfortably nestled in the hill, then reached the parking court and ascended the broad stone staircase to a narrow passage that opened dramatically onto the main courtyard of the house. It was all spine-tinglingly beautiful. We were taken in tow by Wright's secretary, Eugene Masselink, and by senior apprentices Jack Howe and Allen (Davy) Davison, with whom we lunched on chili in the apprentice's dining room. Ronny recalls, "a vibrant small community of young people enthusiastically pursuing their activities; drafting or building/rebuilding at Taliesin, or kitchen and farm duties. And I cannot forget feeling overwhelmed by Mr. Wright's magnificent Asian art objects, the antique oriental rug, and the spectacular rooms."

We learned that Wright had fallen ill and would be unable to spend much time with us. After much touring and talking and note taking, the apprentices assured us that Wright would get a full report of our discussions with them. Although we never met Wright on that visit, we would meet with him roughly ten times over the next few years, once at Taliesin West, four times at the site of our home, and the rest at Wright's suite at the Plaza Hotel in New York City.

Late in February 1951 we received Wright's preliminary drawings for our home, and a few days later, a bill for 5% of $30,000—I don't remember how it got there from $20,000. We had many observations, of which we wrote five pages on March 16:

> Dear Mr. Wright,
>
> We are completely delighted with the beautiful preliminary drawings you've sent us. As we have succeeded in visualizing various aspects of the design our satisfaction has increased.
>
> We sincerely thank you for the prompt attention you have given to our house. You may have heard that there are some people who, while professing admiration for your work,

PRELIMINARY FLOOR PLAN, 1951. *COURTESY THE FRANK LLOYD WRIGHT FOUNDATION, SCOTTSDALE, AZ*

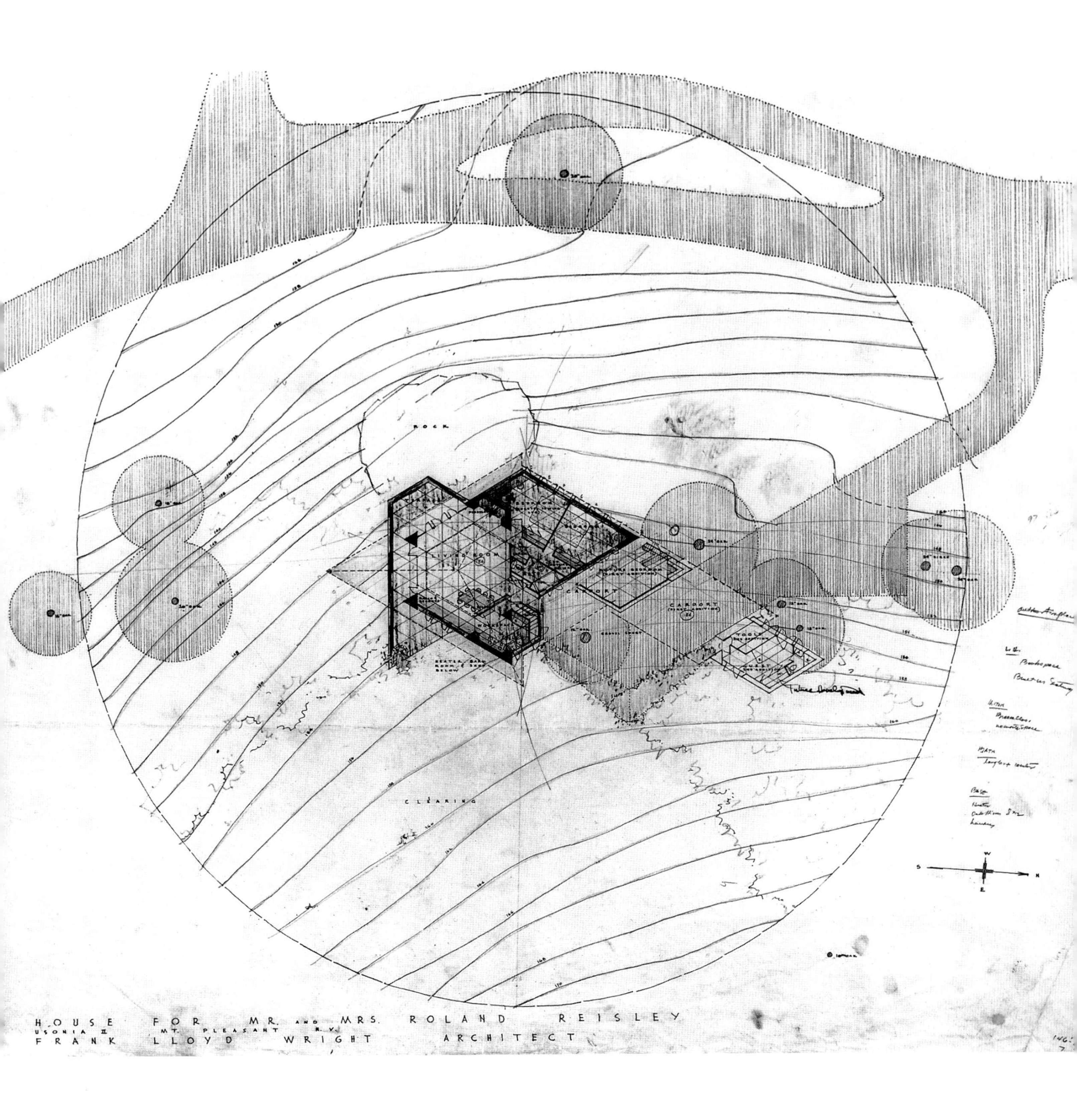
HOUSE FOR MR. AND MRS. ROLAND REISLEY
USONIA II MT. PLEASANT N.Y.
FRANK LLOYD WRIGHT ARCHITECT
ROCK
LIVING ROOM
CARPORT
CLEARING
S
N
W
E

WE HAD MENTIONED THAT WE THOUGHT THE HOUSE WOULD BE AT THE TOP OF THE HILL. "OH NO," WRIGHT SAID. "THAT WOULD JUST BE A HOUSE ON A HILL. TO EXPERIENCE THE HILL, BE OF THE HILL, YOU MUST BUILD INTO IT."

> seem to think that a house of your design involves interminable delays and expenses. We hope that you will enjoy, as did we, the chagrin of the skeptics....
>
> We have enumerated... some comments, questions, and suggestions.

All of these were functional, never stylistic, requests. Among them were book space, built-in furniture, a broom closet, a long sink in the bathroom to facilitate bathing babies, a darkroom, a workshop, a laundry, a wine cellar, and a future maid's room. And we said, "It seems a shame, with so much of the lower level (basement) above ground, not to include some windows. Is there some way this could be done?" In the final drawings Wright accommodated all of these requests. So much for his "disinterest in clients' wishes."

Wright asked for an accurate map of our site's topography, which we sent on April 30, 1951, along with a letter letting him know that we had purchased or optioned various building components, and reiterating "how desperately anxious we are to start building immediately. Our circumstances are such that if we do not proceed almost at once, we may be unable to build at all." We did not think that we were crying wolf, as the Korean War was causing many materials to be less available and more expensive.

WRIGHT PAYS A VISIT

Shortly afterward, on May 13, 1951, Wright visited Usonia and spent several hours with us at our site. Ronny was amazed that Wright, then 84 years old, bounded up the hill so quickly. We discussed plans for the house—mainly the things mentioned in our March 16 letter—and Wright assured us that he would remember the details and that we need not repeat them. He also noted that by slightly shifting the house we would take fuller advantage of the remains of an old road on our land that could be used for the driveway. We had mentioned that we thought the house would be at the top of the hill. "Oh no," Wright said. "That would just be a house on a hill. To experience the hill, be of the hill, you must build into it."

On our drive back to New York City, Wright explained that Jorgine Boomer, the widow of the chairman of the Waldorf-Astoria and the woman for whom he was designing a "cottage" in Phoenix, had insisted he use her apartment—the top of the Waldorf Towers—while some work was being done on his suite at the Plaza. "Come on up. You've got to see this," he told us. It seemed to be two stories high, with four exposures. Photos of crowned heads were on the piano, Della Robbias on the wall. Wright threw the heavy dark drapes up over the valences. "If you're going to live in this city you ought to be able to see it." Showing us the sunken black marble bathtub, he said, "You'll never have something like that!" (We do, only with tan tiles.) We chatted with Wright for a short time, then

PRELIMINARY RENDERING, 1951.

COURTESY THE FRANK LLOYD WRIGHT FOUNDATION, SCOTTSDALE, AZ

TALIESIN SPRING GREEN WISCONSIN

Dear Roland

Mr. Wright has taken quite an interest in your house. As a result I have made 3 new plans in as many days — 4th coming up. So we are far behind the schedule I had laid out to finish in a week. However — it's hot on the boards now — and is turning out a little jewel — a diamond, roughly speaking — sort of what I would call an "original original." Please bear with us! Since everything still has to be done over — we still have a week's solid work ahead of us — possibly 10 days. Will keep you posted — Yrs — Davy Davison

Dear Roland

Your drawings are finally on the way — the Blue Printers will mail them tomorrow — you should get them Monday. This last delay was due to Mr. Wright's not being on hand to sign the drawings — so there wasn't much for us to do but hope and pray you'd be patient till he came back.

The house has received exceptional work and thought — particularly on Mr. Wright's part. It'll be quite a thrill building.

Please keep me posted as work progresses — or if you need help — we want this built right, both from your standpoint & ours.

Sincerely

Davy Davison

Taliesin — Aug 10 '51

CORRESPONDENCE FROM JULY 2, 1951, AND AUGUST 10, 1951. *COLLECTION ROLAND REISLEY*

headed to our own apartment in the city, all the while dreaming of our new home.

A month passed, and we still did not have our final drawings. On June 3, 1951, I wrote to Wright again, essentially urging, "Send drawings. Korean war causing materials shortage." And on July 5 a telegram "RUSH, must have working drawings immediately. Please advise." Although Wright sometimes admonished us to communicate only with him directly, we nevertheless did, at times, write or speak to Masselink or Davison hoping to expedite, or at least find out what was happening. They kept us posted on the progress of our project, which had been delayed somewhat due to Wright's particular interest in it. At last, on August 10, Davison notified us that our plans were on their way. We were extremely happy with these plans, and on August 20 wrote Wright an enthusiastic letter of appreciation, along with some questions about the construction.

> Dear Mr. Wright,
>
> We are extremely happy with the drawings you sent us and are making plans to start construction in the shortest possible time. We have a number of questions concerning details and materials, but will limit ourselves in this letter to the few design problems that must be resolved before we can proceed. . . .

We again questioned extension details, reminded him that he had suggested a minimum deck height of 6 feet 9 inches, rather than 6 feet 6 inches (I am six feet tall), and asked for a substitute for the probably unavailable metal roof. And we asked if he could suggest a builder in this part of the country. We were ready to build.

CONSTRUCTION

It was an exciting, heady time. In the ten months since October 1950, when we first described our needs to Wright, we had studied and commented extensively on the preliminary drawings and we respectfully badgered Wright to make haste. Then in August 1951 we received the working drawings in which virtually all our requests were reflected. We would need some additional changes and we had questions about materials and costs, but we loved the design and were determined to proceed.

Perhaps we should have been frightened, as we did not know who would build the house or what it would actually cost, but somehow we were not. In later years we have guessed that if we had children at the time we might have been less courageous. We were supported by our "family" of Usonians. Before and during the construction of our house Ronny and I spent weekends in Usonia as often as we could. Usonians warmly welcomed us, often inviting us, almost as a matter of course, to share meals or stay overnight on couches or in sleeping bags. The Henkens and Podells were our most frequent hosts.

Most of the homes that had been completed or were under construction in Usonia were built by the Robert Chuckrow Construction Company. Relations with Chuckrow, however, had deteriorated, and so using him did not seem feasible. A prestigious Westchester County builder had expressed interest in working in Usonia. He pointed out that it was very difficult to arrive at a firm price for such an unconventional design, but if we needed one, it would be $100,000. Of course, we thought that ridiculous. Our original $20,000 target had grown to $30,000 and we were thinking that we might manage $35,000. At the time that was a lot of money—and for a

THE PERSONAL ARCHITECTURAL SERVICES OF FRANK LLOYD WRIGHT are available to clients for a fee of ten percent of the cost of the completed building which invariably includes the planting of the grounds and the major furnishings considered as part of the building scheme. The fee is the same for a million dollar building or for a dwelling. The fee is divided in three parts as follows:

1 5% of proposed cost of the building when preliminary studies are presented to the owner. These however, subsequent to original payment, may be modified without additional charge until satisfactory to client and architect.

2 4% additional for the working drawings and specifications payable when in the architect's estimation they are complete and presented ready for bids but with the understanding that should the proposed building costs be more than the client is willing to incur, the architect will do his best to so modify the drawings as to bring costs within reason.

3 1% to complete the fee of ten percent, for the architect's **supervision** only, during construction is payable from time to time during construction or when the building is satisfactorily completed. A final adjustment of the fee according to the total cost of the completed building in order to bring the total fee due the architect to ten percent of completed cost of building, furniture and planting is to be made when requested by the architect. The client in accepting the architect's services agrees that no work in connection with the project shall be executed unless authorized in writing by the architect. The architect's decision in these matters shall be final and binding upon the parties to this agreement. Plans and details are instruments of service only and therefore all remain the property of the architect and all are to be returned to him upon demand.

Superintendence satisfactory to architect and client is to be arranged—if desired—at the client's expense. Traveling expenses incurred by the architect or his agent in direct connection with this work are to be paid from time to time on architect's certificate.

. . . .

The architect, where good general contractors are not available, will undertake to itemize mill work and material for the building, at cost—let contracts to subcontractors for piece work and, so far as possible, eliminate the general contractor by sending a qualified apprentice of the Taliesin Fellowship at the proper time to take charge, do the necessary shopping and hold the entire building operation together. The apprentice will check cost layouts, bids, etc., refer proposed changes to the architect and endeavor to bring the work to successful completion. The lodging and board of this apprentice is to be arranged and paid for by the owner and the necessary traveling expenses of the apprentice are to be paid for by the owner who also pays him at the rate of $50.00 per week for his services so long as he is, in the architect's estimation, required on the work. This arrangement not only saves most of a general contractor's fee but both client and architect are better assured of the results of such simplifications of detail and extensions of space as characterize the new methods of building employed.

. . . .

Before the architect proceeds to design any building an **accurate** topographical survey of the property showing all natural slopes and features such as rock outcroppings, trees, etc., roads, neighboring buildings and service lines for water, sewer, gas and light together with as complete a list of the client's requirements as is feasible, should be on record. Dwelling-houses upon urban lots will not be accepted. Acreage is indispensable.

The services of Frank Lloyd Wright are exclusively owned by The Frank Lloyd Wright Foundation.

TO THE USONIA HOMES: ON ACCOUNT THE REISLEY HOUSE

On account for Working drawings according to conditions of Architectural Services herewith:
4% of $30,000.00, proposed cost: $1,200.00

The Frank Lloyd Wright Foundation
Frank Lloyd Wright, Architect
Taliesin:Spring Green:Wisconsin

September 5,1951

126 West 85 Street
New York 24, N. Y.
October 17, 1951

Mr. Frank Lloyd Wright
Taliesin
Spring Green, Wisconsin

Dear Mr. Wright:

As you know, we have started building our house. Excavation and footings are about complete, the batter boards are up and work is proceeding on the basement.

Several questions have arisen in connection with construction on which we would like your comments. I understand you will be in New York sometime soon and, rather than become involved in lengthy correspondence, we will look forward to discussing them with you when you are here.

You recently sent a bill for our drawings to Usonia Homes. To avoid possible misunderstanding, we assume complete responsibility for any obligations to you in connection with our house. We are most anxious to clear up our account with you as soon as possible.

We are also most anxious to build the house in accordance with your specifications. Unfortunately, the cost of the house is going to be much more than we were prepared for. We will, however, try to swing it. At present, our finances are severely strained to get the house built. You may be sure, however, that we will clear our account very shortly after the house is finished. We hope this arrangement will be agreeable to you.

We trust that you will appreciate the necessity of this arrangement and hope that it will not seriously inconvenience you.

Looking forward to seeing you soon,

Sincerely yours,

Roland Reisley

TALIESIN SPRING GREEN WISCONSIN

Mr. Roland Reisley
126 West 85th Street
New York 24
N. Y.

Dear Roland Reisley: Will see you in New York - but no date set for coming East so far. Probably within next two weeks.

Sincerely,

Frank Lloyd Wright

November 5th, 1951

opposite: INVOICE FROM THE FRANK LLOYD WRIGHT FOUNDATION, SEPTEMBER 5, 1951.

this page: CORRESPONDENCE FROM OCTOBER 17, 1951, AND NOVEMBER 5, 1951.

ALL COLLECTION ROLAND REISLEY

small house. The architects of Usonia insisted that the builders were "robbers" who refused to understand that their designs could be built economically.

Believing that a better-informed builder could satisfy the need, David Henken formed a small team that included some of the master carpenters and masons that had worked for Chuckrow on the earlier Usonia houses. He called his organization Henken Builds. As our friend and Usonia's contact with Wright, Henken was fully acquainted with our project. Davison wanted to supervise the construction, but as Henken was already involved in Usonia and also lived there, he was our logical choice. He could not give us a fixed bid, but promised he would work with us and with Wright to try to bring it in at "not much more than $35,000."

Near the end of September 1951 we started excavating the site and uncovered much more rock than we had expected. Much blasting would be required. Henken noted that if the house were rotated counterclockwise about thirteen degrees, a lot of the blasting could be eliminated with no ill effect to the site planning. We asked Wright about the change, and he agreed to it.

Although we had no children at that time, we expected to enlarge the house and were very concerned about building an addition without having to destroy too much of what we were then building. In our letter of March 16, 1951, we said that we would later need two or three children's bedrooms, a second, perhaps double, bathroom, and if possible some indoor play space. While construction began, we continued to press for details of the future addition. I wrote to Davison, "I'm quite disappointed that Mr. Wright does not feel ready to prepare sketches of future bedrooms at this time.... It seems a shame not to have an integrated design from the outset."

I was concerned about the cost of an addition that had not been planned at the onset. I was also concerned about the costs of the building under construction. Henken shared my concerns, and relayed them in a letter to Wright on November 27. Despite various unresolved questions, we continued to build. One primary concern was the roof and how it might be affected by the extension. David suggested that we make a model of the roof's complex framing to guide the carpenters. I built most of it and it was completed by one of David's draftsmen. We wanted to complete the portion over the living space and defer the carport. We were ready to pour the concrete mat, and so the house had to be weather tight.

Henken wrote to Wright questioning building the fifth section of the roof without knowing how the addition would work with it. He also questioned the strength of the main part of the roof, with only three supports. Wright replied that section five would work into the design of the extension, and that the three supports, recalculated by Wes Peters, were correct. Still we were hesitant to continue, and agreed to meet with Wright in New York in February to discuss the issue.

Wright really wanted to build the roof in metal, but acknowledged its cost and suggested shakes or red stone with battens. He finally agreed to longitudinally applied red asphalt roll material, "temporarily." This would not require the embossed copper fascia, which would save even more money. Wright remarked, "Someday, Roland, when you have the money, put on the copper roof. It will make a gentleman of you." We discussed some alternative fascia detail. I suggested a dentilated fascia and a means to

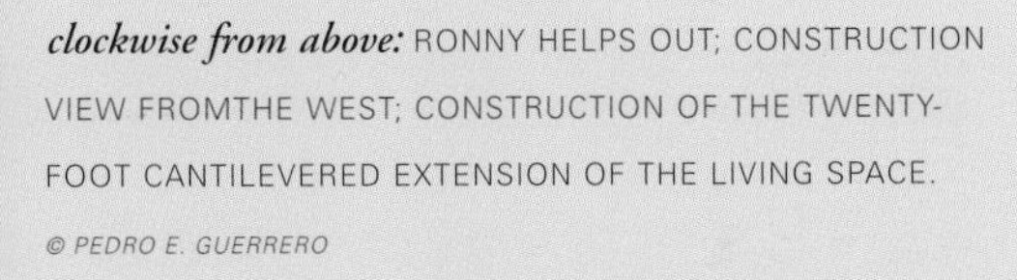

clockwise from above: RONNY HELPS OUT; CONSTRUCTION VIEW FROMTHE WEST; CONSTRUCTION OF THE TWENTY-FOOT CANTILEVERED EXTENSION OF THE LIVING SPACE.

126 West 85 Street
New York 24, N. Y.
December 3, 1951

Mr. Frank Lloyd Wright
Taliesin West
Phoenix, Arizona

Dear Mr. Wright:

As I promised when we last saw you, I am writing to set down our requirements for drawings of the extension to our house.

We will need 3 children's bedrooms, a play area, a large bathroom, a powder room (lavatory and water closet) near the entry, and would like our carport to accommodate 2 cars. Please try to arrange the play area and one of the bedrooms so that they can be added at a still later date. How we will possibly pay for this (you must have received David Henken's letter regarding costs), I don't know. Yet, I do know that we will somehow manage it.

We would like to complete footings and excavation for the extension right now and had planned to proceed with its construction at a slow pace right after completion of the present construction.

Now, because of the prohibitive building costs here in New York, we are facing the likelihood of having to postpone part of even the present house unless you can suggest some cost reducing changes in the present drawings. You can readily see that if, in proceeding with the extension we had to face costly destruction, or compromise, it would just about break us, if not prevent completion of the living space we will need.

You will recall that when you were examining the model of our roof you agreed that probably the logical place for the future bedrooms is in the present carport area. This carport is one of the expensive parts of the present design and whether you change it to reduce its cost, or in connection with the extension, we will need the drawings in order to proceed.

The weather here has been fine for building and the men are now ready to start on the roof - of course, we would like to have the roof on before the snows. Unfortunately, we didn't have the full cost figures until this week. We don't want to go ahead with the roof now without word from you.

-2-

Please forgive us for putting you on the spot like this, but I know you will appreciate the crisis we're in. I also am sure you want to help us complete this beautiful house exactly as you design it. Could we please have the following just about immediately?

1) Suggestions or redesign to reduce cost of present design by $5,000.

2) Preliminary drawings of extension:
   3 small bedrooms*
   large bathroom
   powder room (lav. and w.c.)
   play area*
   2 car carport
   outdoor storage (garden tools, etc.)
   *play area and 1 of the 3 bedrooms to be added separately.

3) Footing and excavation plan.

4) Details of roof transitions and any other details we will need to proceed without fear of later destruction or inefficiency.

We hope and trust we will hear from you very soon.

Kindest regards,

Roland Reisley

Roland Reisley

P.S. Please don't hesitate to phone us or David Henken if you need any other information.

this page: HOPING TO AVOID LATER COSTLY DESTRUCTION, WE PRESSED FOR EXTENSION DETAILS AND REITERATED OUR CONCERN FOR COSTS, DECEMBER 3, 1951.

opposite: WRIGHT'S RESPONSE, DECEMBER 14, 1951.

ALL COLLECTION ROLAND REISLEY

TALIESIN WEST PHOENIX ARIZONA

Mr. Roland Reisley
126 West 85th Street
New York 24

Dear Roland Reisley: I don't know how "Henken builds" you into a situation of this sc sort. Where was he when you began?

I'll do my best, however, and send on suggestions soon as we are settled here.

Faithfully,

Frank Lloyd Wright

December 14th, 1951

N.B. Henken builds - and by a good deal of evidence also ham-and-eggs three times a day - fornicates and (no doubt) snores. So also does ZAMORE (see enclosed).

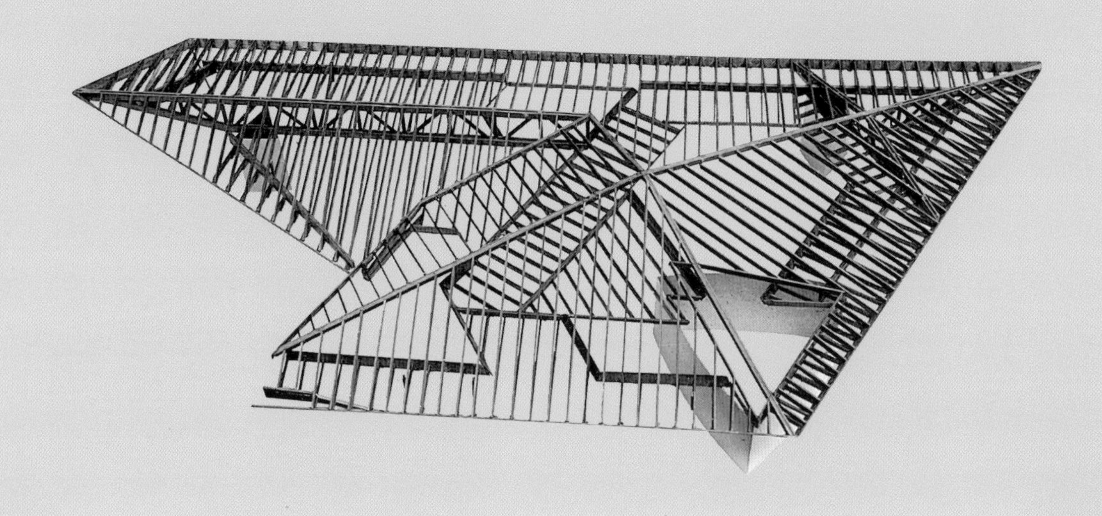

Dear Mr. Wright:

I have not received any answer as yet to my last letter. We have proceeded with the roof design on the Reisley house as last indicated, and have practically completed the shaded triangles, #1, #2, and #3 as shown on the rough sketch. We should finish portion #4 this week, and commence sheathing, but we are stymied until we receive your sketch of how you intend to change portion #5 to accommodate the future bedrooms. THIS IS URGENT!

top: THIS MODEL OF THE COMPLEX ROOF FRAMING HELPED THE CARPENTERS TO UNDERSTAND IT.

bottom: LETTER FROM HENKEN TO WRIGHT, JANUARY 2, 1952.

COLLECTION ROLAND REISLEY

mill it inexpensively. He revised the angles and dimensions, and we used it. Many years later I seriously contemplated "gentlemanly status," but the copper roof would have required changing the fascia. Because it has been so recognizable a feature of the house for so long, we decided to stay with it.

Even with this savings, the house was going to cost more than we expected, and we pressed Wright to find additional ways of reducing its cost. He pointed out that using stone for the exterior walls was expensive and suggested using concrete block, which, he assured us, could produce a very satisfactory result. But we loved the beauty of the stone and sense of solidity. "Well," he said, "stretch yourself. Building this house is one of the best things you'll ever do. Stop for a while, if you must. I promise you'll thank me." We certainly do.

Key craftsmen in building our house were master carpenters Jack Dennerlein and Harry Ackerly and mason Nick Sardelli. They had worked on other houses in Usonia and so were familiar with materials and some of the unusual details, such as compound angles and scribing to stone. They also knew and appreciated that they were working on significant buildings. Sardelli's expertise was in laying brick and smooth troweled concrete floors. He had not worked in stone. But he had watched Wright intently as he showed masons how he wanted the stone work done on the Friedman house. Henken had engaged a fine stone mason to work on our house and tried to have him use a more natural, less formal style. The mason quit and Sardelli volunteered. Without another word of advice, he did a magnificent job integrating stone blasted from our site with granite from the quarry a few miles away. The stone work was admired by Wright and many others.

top: ROOF UNDERCONSTRUCTION. *© PEDRO E. GUERRERO*

bottom: ROOF COMPLETED.

Where possible we tried to help with the construction. I put up the cypress siding on one wall, an easy one, and sanded and applied finish to some of the wood. Ronny filled most of the nail holes with plastic wood. Together we stapled insulation between rafters. Everything was coming together.

MOVING IN

Finally, in June 1952, we moved into our unfinished house. I wrote to Wright: "The house is slowly but surely getting into finished shape and, although living here during the building process is at times uncomfortable, it is nevertheless an increasingly beautiful experience to live here."

A few weeks later Wright visited us. Ronny recalls: "I was always nervous when Mr. Wright visited. What would I offer him to eat or drink, especially when the water was shut off? But he was always gracious and complimentary to me, telling me how I was taking good care of the house." Approaching the house, Wright remarked, "Those chimneys are two feet short." He was right. The masonry was very expensive and Henken thought the chimneys were high enough. But Wright, after all, had some experience with chimneys and knew they should be higher than the roof peak. (We added the two feet a few years later.) Wright asked how the fireplaces worked. We said, "Sort of OK." He replied, "Well, those two feet will help, but you'll want a grate to get the fire off the floor. We often don't draw them, as it might make the house seem expensive." In what has become a rather famous photo by Pedro (Pete) Guerrero, Wright is drawing the grate at a plywood work table in our living room. Other photos that Guerrero took on Wright's visit have also been widely seen, and several are included in this book.

We essentially had no furniture at the time. Ronny bought a simple outdoor table and chairs at Gimbels and was apologetic that it was not of a fancy name brand. Before leaving Wright admired it and asked if we could get him some of the chairs. Ronny discounted the request as flattery, knowing that he appreciated young women. Six weeks later, however, he telegraphed, "Where are the chairs?" I sent him a dozen and saw them years later in photos at Taliesin West. When wealthy clients, the Raywards and then the Hoffmans, who were building nearby, asked about outdoor furniture, Wright told them to "see the Reisleys." A few years ago at Taliesin, we told the story and asked if any chairs remained. Indira Berndtson recalled, "Oh yes it was Mrs. Wright's favorite," and brought one to photograph with us. It had been painted Cherokee red and given a bright blue cushion.

Following Wright's visit, Davison wrote to Henken: "Mr. Wright likes the house. Good for you! I think you're doing a wonderful job."

BUILDING THE ADDITION

In 1954 we received drawings for an addition. We were astonished. Wright apparently had not recorded our house's rotation on our site. The addition, rather than rising into the hill, would have projected, unsupported, over the driveway. I wrote to Wright immediately. Wright visited us with Taliesin associate Wes Peters and agreed that his drawing was not usable. They walked around, stern faced and silent, and asked us to send an accurate new map of the topography.

By June 28, 1955, when we still did not have revised plans, I wrote to Wright:

top: VIEW FROM THE WEST.

bottom: VIEW FROM THE SOUTHWEST.

NINETY-SIX TRIANGULAR LIGHT BOXES AND INDIRECT FLUORESCENT FIXTURES PROVIDE FLEXIBLE LIGHTING THROUGHOUT THE HOUSE. THE CARPET WAS DESIGNED BY MILDRED RESNICK AND RONNY IN 1961. *© ROLAND REISLEY WITH KAREN HALVERSON*

> We are now in a position to continue work on our house to complete it.... With our new baby sharing our bedroom and the first child using the study I'm sure you can appreciate our needs to get the extension built.... During your visit we said that... we are particularly anxious that the extension be at the same level as the present structure. And that we would like to minimize destruction of the existing house as far as possible.... I can't help feeling the design of an extension of consistent architectural quality, that also satisfies our needs, will not be so easy—even for you.... I don't want to be too dramatic, but with the children crowded and waking us at all hours we're really quite desperate. Please let us hear from you soon.

In September I telegraphed, "anxiously awaiting extension drawings," but still received no word. Finally in January 1956 we received preliminary drawings that met virtually all of our requirements. By rearranging the land a bit, in ways we had not imagined, Wright gave us exactly what we asked for. I replied: "We have become so accustomed to expecting the extension to be in the vicinity of the carport that we were little stunned by the location you have chosen. I am, however, very happy to tell you that after having 'lived' with the drawings for a while we are quite enthusiastic over your proposed solution." We continued with three pages of functional comments and questions. They were all accepted and reflected in the working drawings that followed. At last, in the spring of 1957, in time for the birth of our third child, we moved into the extension.

Indeed, the house cost much more than expected, but we survived it and, as Wright predicted, it repaid us with the beauty and quality of our surroundings. After fifty years there, I have realized that there was not a single day when I did not see something beautiful in the space around me. Ronny, too, has said: "My appreciation of the house has grown with time. In early years I did not see and respond to what I do now."

Not only has the house worked well for us, but little maintenance expense has been an unexpected bonus. In fifty years the ceiling was painted once, the interior cypress washed and waxed once, the concrete floors need only mopping and very occasional wax, a few joints in the stone walls were repointed and—the roof has not leaked!

Frank Lloyd Wright's towering stature as an architect brought much interest in his colorful life and personality. Distorted facts and embellished anecdotes have contributed to a widely accepted, disparaging characterization of Wright as totally self serving, disinterested in his clients' functional needs and budget, and careless about the performance of his designs. Unfortunately, that view has interfered with understanding the significance of Wright's work. I am personally acquainted with many of Wright's clients. Those who built with him recount entirely positive experiences, while many who did not build had complaints.

I AM PERSONALLY ACQUAINTED WITH MANY OF WRIGHT'S CLIENTS. THOSE WHO BUILT WITH HIM RECOUNT ENTIRELY POSITIVE EXPERIENCES, WHILE MANY WHO DID NOT BUILD HAD COMPLAINTS.

WESTERN UNION
TELEGRAM
W. P. MARSHALL, PRESIDENT

CLASS OF SERVICE
This is a fast message unless its deferred character is indicated by the proper symbol.

SYMBOLS
DL = Day Letter
NL = Night Letter
LT = International Letter Telegram

The filing time shown in the date line on domestic telegrams is STANDARD TIME at point of origin. Time of receipt is STANDARD TIME at point of destination

A165CC 5C 25 COLLECT

SPRINGGREEN WIS 107PMC SEP 22 1955

ROLAND REISLEY, BURLINGAME ASSOCIATES

AN ANS NL 21ST FAX GFC NYK EMD

IMPOSSIBLE SEND PRELIMINARIES UNTIL WE HAVE COMPLETE INFORMATION CONCERNING WHERE PRESENT HOUSE IS LOCATED AND WHERE THE GRADES ARE KINDLY AIR MAIL. BEST REGARDS.

FRANK LLOYD WRIGHT

835P

THE COMPANY WILL APPRECIATE SUGGESTIONS FROM ITS PATRONS CONCERNING ITS SERVICE

Bear Ridge Road
Pleasantville, N. Y.
May 18, 1953

Mr. Frank Lloyd Wright
Taliesin
Spring Green, Wisconsin

Dear Mr. Wright,

Since your last visit with us nearly a year ago, we have done a little more work on the interior of our house, but, except for the outside ceilings, have done virtually nothing on the exterior. We are desperately anxious to continue with the exterior. There is alot of masonry to be done around the carport; we sadly need a driveway; much cleaning, grading, backfilling and planting is needed. We can do none of these without, at least, the preliminary drawings of the extension that you have promised. Our first child is due this fall and the extension will be sorely needed.

Won't you please send these drawings out to us right away so that we can discuss any questions on them with you when you come to New York at the end of this month? We will look forward to hearing from you.

With kind regards,

Roland Reisley

Roland Reisley

WESTERN UNION
TELEGRAM
W. P. MARSHALL, PRESIDENT

DOMESTIC SERVICE
Check the class of service desired; otherwise this message will be sent as a fast telegram
TELEGRAM
DAY LETTER
NIGHT LETTER

INTERNATIONAL SERVICE
Check the class of service desired; otherwise the message will be sent at the full rate
FULL RATE
LETTER TELEGRAM
SHORE-SHIP

1206 (4-55)

NO. WDS.-CL. OF SVC.	PD. OR COLL.	CASH NO.	CHARGE TO THE ACCOUNT OF	TIME FILED

Send the following message, subject to the terms on back hereof, which are hereby agreed to

September 10th, 1956

FRANK LLOYD WRIGHT

WE WOULD LIKE TO START EXTENSION IMMEDIATELY BUT NEED YOUR HELP ON SEVERAL PROBLEMS. COULD YOU VISIT US FOR A SHORT TIME WHEN YOU ARE IN NEW YORK. REGARDS

ROLAND REISLEY

Will call you Roland – when in N.Y. There in about 10 days.

F.Ll.W.

---

this page, clockwise from above: MAY 18, 1953, I AGAIN REQUEST DRAWING OF EXTENSION; SEPTEMBER 22, 1955, AFTER NOTING THE BUILDING'S ROTATION, WRIGHT NEEDED AN ACCURATE NEW "TOPO"; SEPTEMBER 10, 1956, THE NEW DRAWING IS RECEIVED. *ALL COLLECTION ROLAND REISLEY*

opposite top: PRELIMINARY FLOOR PLAN OF ADDITION, 1956.

opposite bottom: PRELIMINARY RENDERING OF ADDITION, 1956.

BOTH COURTESY THE FRANK LLOYD WRIGHT FOUNDATION, SCOTTSDALE, AZ

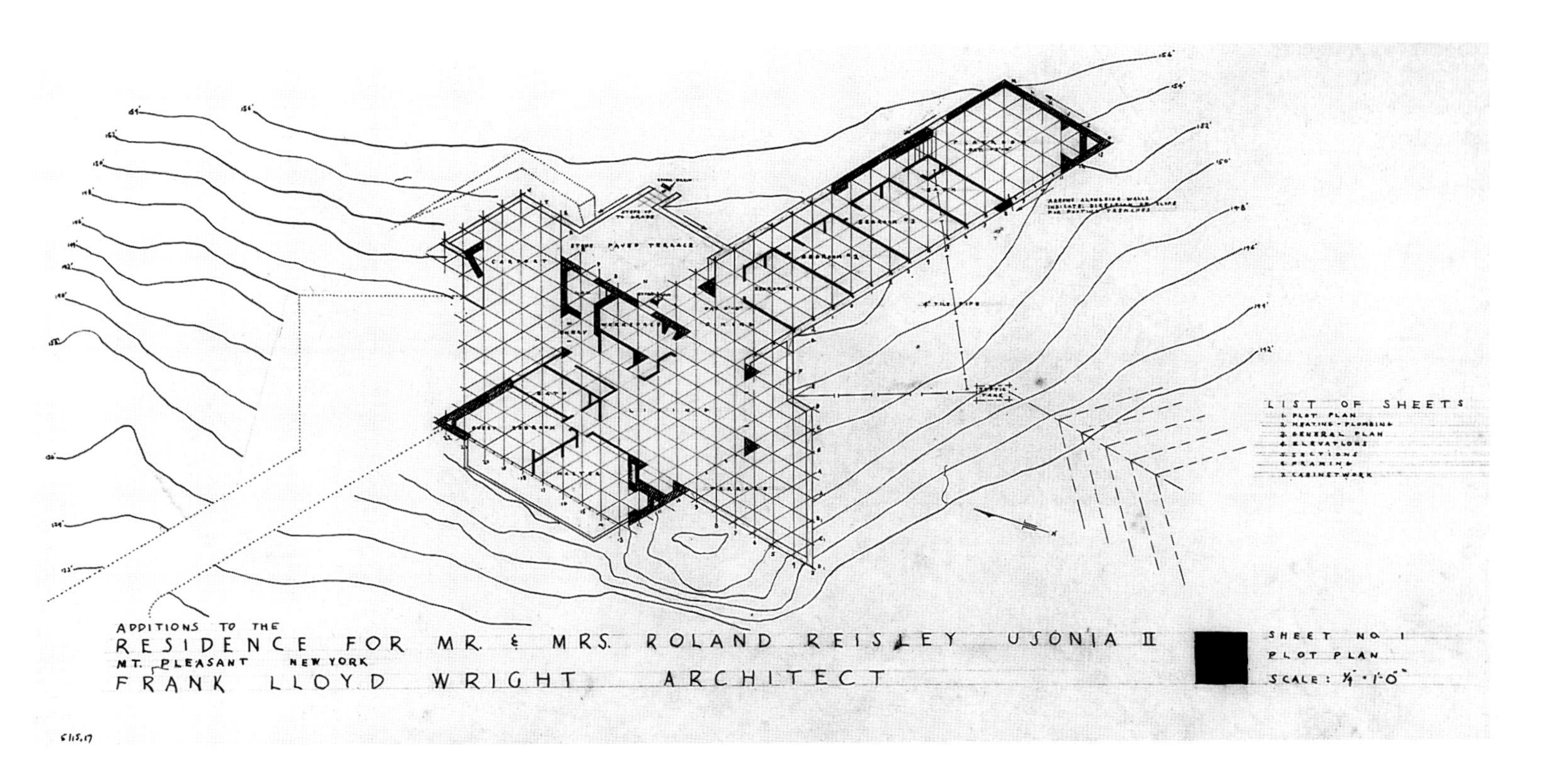
LIST OF SHEETS
1. PLOT PLAN
2. HEATING - PLUMBING
3. GENERAL PLAN
4. ELEVATIONS
5. SECTIONS
6. FRAMING
7. CABINETWORK
ADDITIONS TO THE
RESIDENCE FOR MR. & MRS. ROLAND REISLEY USONIA II
MT. PLEASANT NEW YORK
FRANK LLOYD WRIGHT ARCHITECT
SHEET NO. 1
PLOT PLAN
SCALE: 1/4"=1'-0"
5115.17

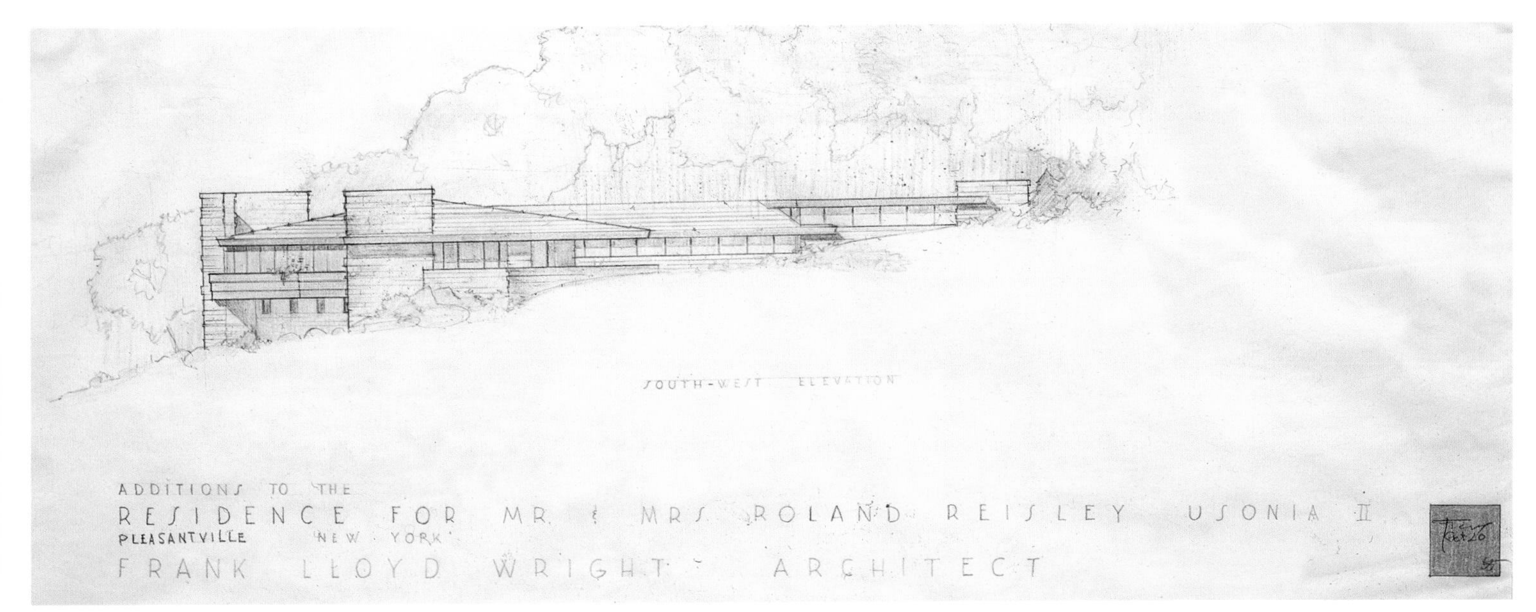
SOUTH-WEST ELEVATION
ADDITIONS TO THE
RESIDENCE FOR MR. & MRS. ROLAND REISLEY USONIA II
PLEASANTVILLE NEW YORK
FRANK LLOYD WRIGHT - ARCHITECT

REMEMBERING WRIGHT

My memories of my many meetings with Wright are only good. Ronny agrees: "He was always warm and responsive to me. I resent it when some historians say that Wright's clients were dominated by his personality. I was 'dominated' by the work, the artistry—not personality. It is fair to note Wright's concentration, his focus on whatever he was doing. In conversation, he listened and spoke with interest."

I particularly remember one meeting during the design of my home. Though determined to discuss my list of concerns, my demeanor was extremely deferential, "hat-in-hand," 27-year-old in the presence of "God." Wright sensed this and said, "Roland, sit down. You're the client. I'm your architect. It's my job to give you a design that satisfies your needs. If you are not satisfied, I'll keep working until you are. But you must tell me. Otherwise—take what you get."

I was dismayed when Brendan Gill paraphrased me in his book *Many Masks,* and went on to write, "Reisley, then in his twenties, could scarcely believe his ears; if he had been ten years older and twice as self-confident, no doubt he would have elicited a very different response." Gill, however, observed that "Wright liked designing for young people; one can think of fifty couples whom Wright worked with and befriended, including the Hannas, the Jacobses, and the Reisleys." Perhaps older clients had stylistic convictions and were less open to Wright's ideas. Wright once mentioned to me that he should be working on larger projects, not houses, but that he loved doing them and could not stop.

I feel privileged to have had this relationship with Wright, which extended beyond his work on my house and gave me insights into his working methods. I was with Wright at the site of the Guggenheim Museum when the foundation was being built. He was meeting representatives of the New York City agency concerned with building codes. Wright had specified clear glass in the skylight over the museum's rotunda. The city said it was not rated to carry the required snow load, and so industrial wired glass must be used. Wright disliked that glass and proposed a translucent corrugated material of plastic or fiberglass. A "shootout" had been arranged. Large sheets of the plastic and wired glass were supported at each end and a required number of sand bags were loaded on the centers. Five or six of us were standing near the edge of the site, noting that the glass was sagging about six inches and the plastic more than twelve inches. "There you are," said the city men when, like a thunderbolt, the glass exploded. So they used the wired glass. Stronger clear glass became available later and it was used in the recent renovation of the museum.

In 1959, during the completion of the Guggenheim and not many years after that of our home, Frank Lloyd Wright died at the age of 92. Though saddened, of course, we also felt lucky to have known him and to have the home he designed. And we commiserated with the many apprentices with whom we had become friends, who truly loved him. But it would take many more years to increasingly appreciate the impact on our lives of the timeless beauty of the environment he gave us.

FRANK LLOYD WRIGHT AT THE REISLEY HOUSE, 1952.

left: RONNY, BARBARA, AND LINC REISLEY WITH FRANK LLOYD WRIGHT, SUMMER 1956, AT THE REISLEY HOUSE.
above: ROLAND, ROB, LINC, RONNY, AND BARBARA REISLEY AT THEIR HOME.
opposite: ROLAND AND RONNY REISLEY WITH THEIR FRIEND, RAKU ENDO, IN THEIR LIVING ROOM, 1999. ENDO, A FORMER WRIGHT APPRENTICE AND ARCHITECT/PRESERVATIONIST IN JAPAN, IS THE SON OF ARATO ENDO, WHO WORKED WITH WRIGHT ON THE IMPERIAL HOTEL IN TOKYO. *SATOMI SAKURAI*

INDEX OF USONIA'S HOMES

Usonia's homes and the original families who built them are listed in this section. At this writing, in 2001, members of twenty-four of the original forty-seven families continue to live in Usonia. The chronological listing is not precise, but corresponds to the period of design, construction, and occupancy of each house. Some of the photographs are historic, while others are contemporary.

The site numbers listed herein are those that were assigned to the original circular site plan and retained on the revised 1955 site plan (shown on the facing page), when all sites were enlarged to 1.25 acres. After the roads were improved, the post office assigned new street addresses to the homes. The shaded areas indicate community land of Usonia Homes–A Cooperative, Inc.

WESTCHESTER COUNTY LAND RECORDS

David Henken House, 1949, by David Henken
Site 34
David (engineer/architect) and Priscilla (teacher)
joined Usonia 7/2/44
Children Jonathan, Meriamne, and Elissa
© PEDRO E. GUERRERO

Odif Podell House, 1949, by David Henken
Site 32
Odif (engineer) and Judeth (social service secretary)
joined Usonia 7/2/44
Children Joshua, Ethan, and Tamara
COSMO-SILEO ASSOCIATES

Aaron Resnick House, 1949, by Aaron Resnick
Site 52
Aaron (engineer/architect) and Mildred (art teacher/artist)
joined Usonia 12/28/45
Children Lucy and Jessie
COSMO-SILEO ASSOCIATES

Sidney Benzer House, 1949, by Aaron Resnick
Site 51
Sidney (dentist) and Florence (jewelry artist)
joined Usonia 1/27/47
Children Ted, Michael, Karen, and Debbie

Brandon House, 1949, by David Henken
Site 18
Herbert (trade paper publisher) and Ada
joined Usonia 2/6/47
Children Bob and Carl

Kepler House, 1949, by David Henken
Site 19
John (wood craftsman) and Jean
joined Usonia 5/28/47
Children Michael, Kendy, and Chris

Watts House, 1949, by Schweikher & Elting
Site 49
Rowland (labor/public-interest lawyer) and Fay (union leader) joined Usonia 12/5/47
Children David, Linda, and Lanny

Bier House, 1949, by Kaneji Domoto
Site 53
Arthur (physician) and Gertrude
joined Usonia 3/30/48
Children Irene and Susan
Occupied since 1972 by Marvin and Johanna Cooper and their children Nancy, Lauren, and Alyssa
COURTESY BIER FAMILY

Lurie House, 1949, by Kaneji Domoto
Site 31
Jesse Z. (journalist) and Irene
joined Usonia 6/22/48
Children Ellen and Susan

Harris House, 1949, by Kaneji Domoto
Site 26
William (engineer) and Esther
joined Usonia 6/25/48
Children Ethan, Joel, Michael, and Naomi

Wax House, 1950, by Aaron Resnick
Site 24
Jack (magazine editor) and Anne
joined Usonia 7/14/48
Children Barbara and Steven

Brody House, 1951, by David Henken
Site 8
George (accountant) and Julia (librarian)
joined Usonia 4/2/45

Friedman House, 1950, by Frank Lloyd Wright
Site 14
Sol (owner of book and music stores) and Bertha
joined Usonia 1/20/48
Children Robert, Richard, and David
Occupied after 1970 by Michael and Maria Osheowitz
and their children Tania and Melitta

Masson House, 1951, by David Henken
Site 45
John (insurance salesman) and Ruth
joined Usonia 11/18/46
Child Jack

Gabel House, 1951, by Aaron Resnick
Site 46
Murry (insurance broker) and Gertrude (art teacher)
joined Usonia 4/22/46
Children Jonathan, Laura, Michael, and Matthew
The original basic Usonian house was later "building contractor remodeled."

Victor House, 1951, by Aaron Resnick
Site 29
Max (importer) and Trude
joined Usonia 6/16/48
Children Ursula and Hannah
© PEDRO E. GUERRERO

Sidney Miller House, 1951, by Aaron Resnick
Site 30
Sidney (textile executive) and Barbara (librarian)
joined Usonia 7/12/48
Children Paul, Bruce, Ricky, and Adam

Scheinbaum House, 1951, by Ted Bower
Site 9
Al (book dealer) and Lucille (teacher)
joined Usonia 7/20/48
Children Ann and Irene

Silson House, 1951, by Kaneji Domoto
Site 43
John (physician) and Dorothy (nurse)
joined Usonia 7/28/48
Child Peter

Hillesum House, 1951, by Aaron Resnick
Site 33
Jacob (diamond cleaver) and Lisette (seamstress)
joined Usonia 8/9/48
Child Joey
COURTESY HILLESUM FAMILY

Glass House, 1951, by Ted Bower
Site 37
Edward (furniture executive) and Istar (interior designer and dancer) joined Usonia 8/17/48
Child Betsy

Anderson House, 1951, by David Henken
Site 6
James (chemist) and Marjorie (teacher)
joined Usonia 8/24/48
Children Susan and Peter

Lew House, 1951, by Schweikher & Elting
Site 42
Isaiah (dentist) and Charlotte
joined Usonia 10/14/48
Children Alan, Jason, and Carol
© PEDRO E. GUERRERO

Auerbach House, 1951, by Aaron Resnick
Site 44
Irwin (auditor) and Ottalie (dietician)
joined Usonia 12/6/48
The house was demolished in 1997.All that remains is the fireplace shown here.

Silver House, 1952, by David Henken
Site 10
Kenneth (professor) and Janet (teacher)
joined Usonia 2/28/51
Children Gail and Bill

Milner House, 1952, by David Henken
Site 4
Robert (newspaper distributor) and Bess
joined Usonia 4/11/51
Children Hope and Lee
The houses was later extended (right) by Aaron Resnick for Hope and her husband Merrill Sobie.

Robertson House, 1952, by David Henken
Site 7
John (professor) and Janet
joined Usonia 7/15/51
Children Jack and Marjory

Parker House, 1952, by Warner & Leeds
Site 5
James (publishing executive) and Virginia
joined Usonia 11/1/51
Children Bruce and Carol

Harry Miller House, 1952, by George Nemeny
Site 21
Harry (sporting goods distributor) and Winifred
joined Usonia 11/1/51
Children Tom, Patsy, and Ken

Tamlyn House, 1953, by Aaron Resnick
Site 3
Walter (engineer) and Jean
(remarried to Ann)
joined Usonia 7/8/52
Children Robert, Ralph, and Jane

Scheiner House, 1955, by Warner & Leeds
Site 47
Martin (engineer) and Jane
joined Usonia 7/7/54

Zais House, 1955, Tech-Bilt
Site 39
Arnold (engineer) and Bette (social worker)
joined Usonia 8/3/54
Children Adam and Gregory

Grayson House, 1955, by Tobias Goldstone
Site 12
Ted (business owner) and Frances
joined Usonia 7/7/54

Caro House, 1956, by Aaron Resnick
Site 23
Ulrich (engineer) and Gloria
joined Usonia 2/24/55
Children Debbie, Jani, and Alan

Siegel House, 1956, by Kaneji Domoto
Site 17
Robert (lawyer and executive) and Norma
joined Usonia 5/17/55
Children Joanne and Peter

Berman House, 1957, by Ulrich Franzen
Site 58
Steven (business executive) and Ellen (social worker)
joined Usonia 6/28/55
Children Douglas, Roger, and Todd

Millman House, 1957, Tech-Bilt
Site 25
Irving (steel salesman) and Gloria
joined Usonia 11/29/56
Children Steven and Beth
The house pictured was completely rebuilt in 1998, retaining much of the Henken remodeling (see page 100).

Samuel Resnick House, 1958, by Aaron Resnick
Site 57
Samuel (business owner) and Amy (social worker)
joined Usonia 5/8/56
Children Johanna, Leslie, Jonathan, and Maxanne

Paul Benzer House, 1958, by Aaron Resnick
Site 1
Paul (dentist) and Rita (social worker)
joined Usonia 1958
Children Marcy and Judie

Jerry Podell House, 1959, by David Henken
Site 13
Jerry (lawyer) and Charlotte
joined Usonia 1958
Children Lisa, Eric, Stephanie, and Sara
Lower level addition by Peter Gluck for the Lieberman family.

Hirsch House, 1960, by David Leavitt
Site 55
Hyman (stockbroker) and Deborah (psychotherapist)
joined Usonia 6/20/59
Children Amy, Roger, and Jordan

Kahn House, 1962, by Aaron Resnick
Site 11
Roger (author) and Joan (social worker)
joined Usonia 3/13/62
Child Gordon
Occupied since 1963 by Mel and Edith Smilow and their children
Pamela and Judy

Lerner House, 1964, by Lawrence Lerner
Site 50
Lawrence (interior designer) and Leslie
joined Usonia 5/21/63
Child Eric

Bier House II, 1969, pre-fab
When Arthur retired, the Biers left their home in Usonia (see page 157) for Cape Cod. They missed Usonia, and wanted to return, but no sites were available. They built this house on a site adjacent to Usonia, and returned as members. Successive owners have extended the house.

Eickelbeck House, 1994 addition by Michael Wu
Site 35
The house was remodeled from the Benjamin Henken House (see pages 51, 99, and 155).

Akselrod/Resnick House, 1997, by Peter Wiederspahn
Site 44
The family bought the Auerbach House, 1951. Prevented by wetland restrictions from enlarging it, they had to demolish it (see page 165) and build higher on the site.

Margulies House, 2000 remodeling by Sven Armstad
Site 9
The house was remodeled from the Scheinbaum House (see page 161). This remodeling is sympathetic to the original.